Preface

When you visit Strata Florida for the first time you can appreciate immediately that the place is special, nestled by two rivers on the last patch of level, fertile ground before the mountains begin to rise to the east. But to make full sense of the land's history you may need some help. That is what this book aims to supply.

For the first time the whole story of Strata Florida – the prehistoric cairns, wells and forts, the Cistercian abbey and its great estates, and Mynachlog Fawr, the seventeenth-century farm built out of the abbey's stones – is summarised by its leading authority, Professor David Austin. For decades David has used all his archaeological and historical skills to explore Strata Florida, and uncover and interpret evidence about it. This summary of his work meets a long-felt need, and we are very grateful to him for preparing it.

This book is the second in a series published by the Strata Florida Trust that aims to use the latest research to explain different aspects of the site. The Strata Florida Trust is a registered charity, with two aims: to restore Mynachlog Fawr and its farm buildings, and to use them to create a Strata Florida Centre for people to learn about archaeology and conservation, Welsh culture and history, and the natural environment.

We hope you enjoy reading the book. If you would like to know more, or to help support our work in this remarkable place, we should be pleased to hear from you.

Andrew Green
Chair, Strata Florida Trust

DEDICATION
The author dedicates this book to his wife, Gaenor Parry, who has been a constant support and inspiration through the whole life of the project.

An overview

Fig. 1: The site of Strata Florida with the monastic church outline in the centre, maintained by Cadw, the parish church of St Mary and its cemetery in the foreground, and the farm buildings of Mynachlog Fawr owned by the Strata Florida Trust beyond.

Fig. 2: The fourteenth-century head of the full-length effigy of the Lord Rhys in St David's Cathedral.

Strata Florida is the site of a former Cistercian monastery which was of immense importance to Wales during the Middle Ages (Fig. 1). Even today the place, its history and landscapes, have great significance for Welsh people and their culture. First founded in 1164, it was in 1184 re-founded by the Lord Rhys (yr Arglwydd Rhys), Prince of Deheubarth, who gave it extensive lands and an ambitious purpose (Fig. 2). It was always regarded with suspicion by the English Crown for its support of Welsh identity and independence, and after its heyday in the 13th century the abbey was gradually reduced in size. It was finally closed during Henry VIII's Dissolution of the monasteries in 1539.

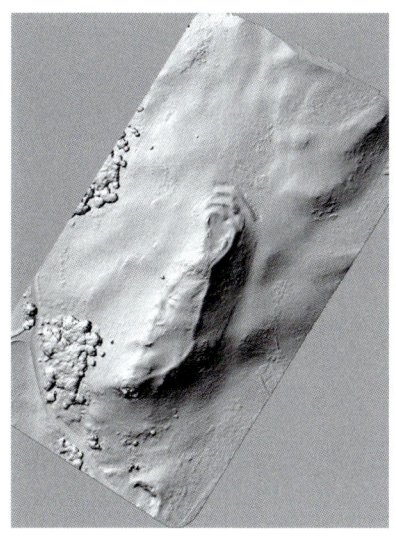

Fig. 3: Photogrammetric vertical image of Pen-y-bannau ('Head of the peaks') hillfort which lies on a ridge just to the north of Strata Florida.

Yet this well-known story of Strata Florida is much longer and greater. It stretches back over 4000 years to the time when early human settlers began to establish farms. Even then the present location of Strata Florida seems to have been a sacred place, a point in the landscape where connections could be made between the spiritual and material worlds. Farming landscapes developed and filled with people and their societies, and economies became more complex and structured. By the later Iron Age the landscape was as open as it is today with complex communities and tribal hierarchies, reflected in the large number of hill-forts they built on the hills around Strata Florida (Fig. 3)

This Celtic world continued largely uninterrupted, even during the brief and limited military intervention of the Romans (c. A.D. 80 – c. 150). Climatic deterioration and plague brought set-backs as the region emerged into the early Middle Ages (the 'Dark Ages'), but by the eighth and ninth centuries A.D. new confederacies and kingdoms had formed and recovery begun. Christianity also arrived, centred on a 'Celtic' form of monasticism, including possibly at Strata Florida itself. This provided the platform for the arrival of the reformed Cistercians from Catholic Christendom, following in the wake of the Anglo-Norman assault on the independent princedoms of Wales.

After the Dissolution, the abbey's long history and its complex spiritual and cultural meanings survived and remain embedded within this sacred landscape. For nearly 200 years the increasingly ruined abbey was the centre of a gentry estate, run by the Stedman family, created out of part of the former lands of Strata Florida. They lived in and amongst the decaying architectures, from time to time putting up their own buildings, some of which still stand today (Fig. 4).

Fig. 4: The house of Mynachlog Fawr (Great Abbey) built in 1670-80 by the Stedman family and now owned by the Strata Florida Trust.

After the mid-eighteenth century the estate came into the hands of more distant gentry and the buildings were occupied by tenant farmers. By 1870 the tenants were the Arch family who still farm the land today, and by the mid-twentieth century they had bought the freehold (Fig. 5).

Fig. 5: The Arch family in the kitchen of the house where the two brothers, Charles (far left) and Dai (centre left), were brought up.

It was from the Arches that the Strata Florida Trust bought Mynachlog Fawr in 2016 and began the task of conserving and converting it into a Centre for visitors, research and education, all predicated on the achievements of the people who have lived and worked in this extraordinary landscape for thousands of years.

Location and landscape

Strata Florida lies to the east of the village of Pontrhydfendigaid on the B4343 between Tregaron and Aberystwyth. The remains of the former monastery are to be found among the western ridges of the Cambrian Mountains, the north-south upland plateau which divides east from west in central Wales (Fig. 6).

The Cambrians are higher in the north around Pumlumon than in the south where they die away westwards into the Preselau range. Behind Strata Florida they rise to just over 1700 feet (500 metres) above sea level. From these hills spring a number of rivers, some flowing westwards into the Irish Sea (Cardigan Bay) and some east and south into the Bristol Channel. One of these is the Afon Teifi which flows out of the hills to the west from its main source at Teifi Pools before turning south into Cors Caron (Tregaron Bog) and then flowing out into the Irish Sea at Cardigan. In the vicinity of Strata Florida, the Teifi is joined on the south side by its tributary the Afon Glasffrwd coming from its own source at Blaenglasffrwd. Both rivers run in steep-sided gullies down the flanks of the Cambrians, before settling into a more meandering course to north and south of the abbey's original precinct (Fig. 7).

Fig. 6: The location of Strata Florida in central Wales. To the east and south of it are the Cambrian Mountains with the valleys of other major rivers, the Wye, Severn and Tywi, flowing from them. To the west are the upper Teifi and Aeron valleys and the Mynydd Bach, a range of low coastal hills. To the north the valleys of the Ystwyth and Rheidol cut into the increasingly high Cambrians which eventually lead into the true mountains of Snowdonia.

Fig. 7: An eastwards view of the abbey's immediate environs. In the centre foreground are the flat good grasslands beneath which lie the extensive archaeological remains of the large precinct of the abbey when it was set out soon after 1184. To the left (north) is the course of the Afon Teifi flowing from its source in the Cambrian Mountains. To the right is the course of the Afon Glasffrwd, its line marked by trees in the foreground, next to Abbey Wood with beyond, the trees planted by the Forestry Commission in the 1950s.

In terms of Strata Florida's local landscape, there are four main types, each with their long histories of use leaving traces which can still be seen and mapped today (Fig. 8).

1. To the west is the raised bog of Cors Caron (Fig. 9), situated on the flat glaciated floor of the Teifi valley. This was much larger than it is today and we have been able to reconstruct its historic extent (lighter blue on Fig. 8).

Fig. 8: The topography of the Upper Teifi valley environs with the original plan of the re-founded abbey of 1184 picked out in red.

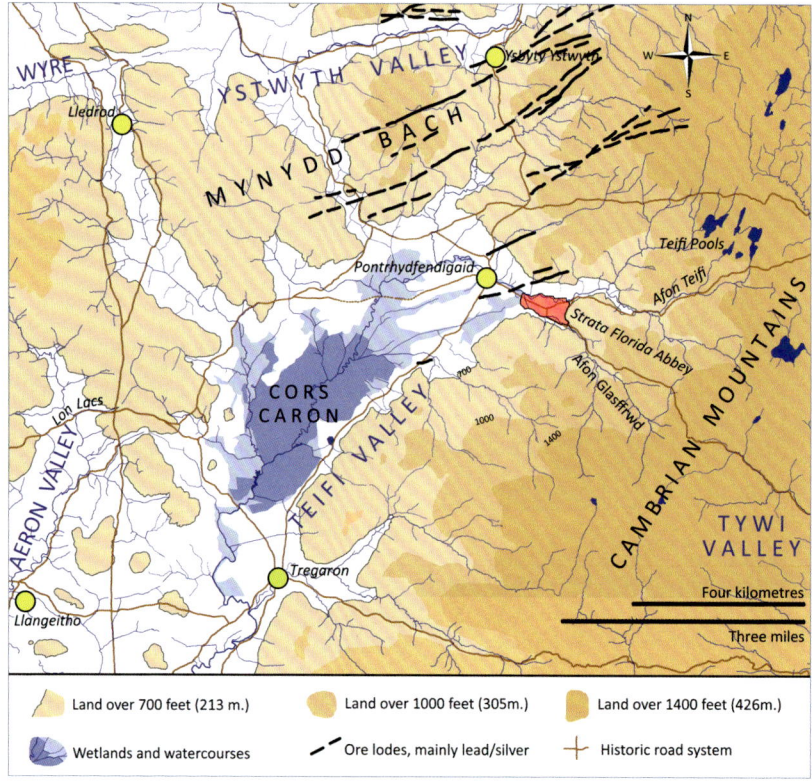

Fig. 9: Bird's eye view of Cors Caron looking northwards towards the snow-capped peak of Pumlumon. The buildings in the foreground are Maes Llyn, one of the abbey farms, probably a place of habitation since the Bronze Age. The evidence for large-scale peat cutting can be seen in the middle distance as linear features — this was, until very recently, a common right for local people as was grazing animals on its surface.

2. Around this (Fig. 10), and above the flood risk, are the good, relatively well-drained and cultivated lands, on which stood the ancient farms. These can also be identified as the *hendref*, the focus of all agricultural management for the kin and their workers, and the places of year-round habitation. This land lies below the 700-foot (215m.) contour and is white on Fig. 8.

Fig. 10: Looking eastwards towards Strata Florida across Cors Caron in the foreground with its fingers of former wetlands dividing the good lands of the ancient farms into better-drained ridges and niches. The nearest farm is Dolbeidiau, one of the ancient farms which became, after the arrival of the Cistercians, a dedicated dairy. The modern settlement of Pontrhydfendigaid, once the abbey's demesne village, is to the left with, beyond, the narrow valley in the Cambrians within which Strata Florida was built.

3. Above this contour and up to approximately 1000 feet (305m.) are the lower slopes of the Cambrian Mountains, known as the *ffridd* in Welsh (Fig. 11). This is land which has changed in use over time. Initially it was a mixed landscape of open pasture interspersed with enclosures where the herds of cattle and other animals were managed as part of a short-distance transhumance system between the *hendref* and the *hafod* ('summer house'). Over time the *ffridd* was colonised, from the later Middle Ages up to the middle years of the nineteenth century, by the creation of farms occupied all year round (Fig. 11).

Fig. 11: The small farms and enclosures of the encroachment onto the ffridd above Ysbyty Ystwyth, land once in the tenure of Strata Florida Abbey. These were farms swept away by the agrarian decline of the later nineteenth century and beyond.

4. Above the thousand-foot contour today are the remnants of the ancient open and rough pastures, the *mynydd*, largely treeless since the Bronze Age and dotted with bogs and peaty mires (Fig. 12). The ancient rights of community access to these commons were eroded by the great estates following the dissolution of the monastery and eventually lost altogether by the twentieth century.

Fig. 12: The mynydd at Troed-y-rhiw to the north-east of the abbey, looking east across the peneplain plateau of the Cambrian Mountains. As far as the eye can see this was part of the great tract of open rough pasture in the possession of Strata Florida, sustaining large sheep flocks. In the foreground is the upper edge of the ffridd where there are earthworks of two small tenant farms as well as those of a monastic bercaria or sheep management centre.

One other, final element to be seen on Fig. 8 is the location of ore veins mostly containing lead, but also silver, copper and (very occasionally) gold. These have been important since the Bronze Age, and among these lodes are a number of sites where the abbey had its mines.

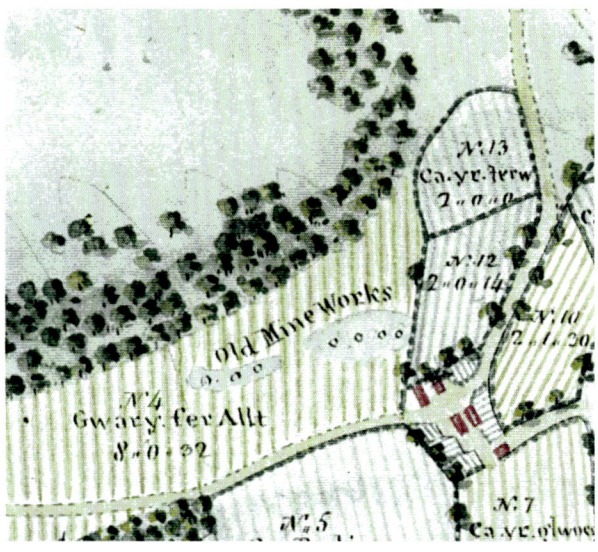

Fig. 13: Just to the north of the abbey precincts is one of the abbey's ancient demesne farms, Bron-y-berllan. On the slope just above the farm there is depicted, on a Powell estate map of 1819, a site of 'old mine works'. Our archaeological study of this site has shown that the line of 7 pits shown are the remains of shallow mine shafts.

Before the abbey

In the long-term climate history of our planet, the present warm episode of our current Ice Age began some 12,000 years ago when the ice sheets began to retreat leaving deposits of moraine in valleys smoothed by glacial action. Fast run-offs from melt-water also left deep gorges like the Afon Glasffrwd cutting into the flanks of the hills (Fig. 14).

Fig. 14: The Afon Glasffrwd in the lower part of its wooded, steep-sided gorge, reminiscent perhaps of a more ancient landscape.

At this time too a great lake of melt-water formed behind a dump of moraine lying across the Teifi, and as it slowly in-filled with silt and peat it became the massive peat bog of Cors Caron. By 10,000 years before the present day (b.p.), all glacial traces had vanished and both vegetation and animals began rapidly to return. The first scrub and tree growth was mostly juniper giving way to birch, with hazel also appearing at c. 9700 b.p. About 500 years later came elm and pine followed quickly by oak all supplanting the birch dominance.

Then, at about 7000 b.p. (that is 5000 B.C.) came a rapid replacement of the pine by alder. It is at about this time too, if not before, that the first humans entered the landscape, perhaps from the start influencing the alder rise by felling the pine. These were Mesolithic hunter-gatherers moving through the landscape in small, probably kin-based, bands in pursuit of the herds of the larger animals, such as deer and wild cattle. This would have been seasonal, working into the hinterland from coastal winter camps such as the Nab Head in Pembrokeshire. It could be that this hunting managed the herds by driving them to kill sites, perhaps along cleared tracks and pathways.

At 5000 b.p. (3000 B.C.), came the decline of elm which is a phenomenon often attributed elsewhere to the advent of Neolithic arable farming and settlement. This is a much debated ecological event, but as far as the region under consideration is concerned there is no clear evidence yet for Neolithic settlement and it might be better explained as the result of a disease similar to modern elm decline, although increased hunter management might also have been involved. At this point blanket peat mires began to form on the rapidly denuded uplands, increasing the acidity of soils, itself further impeding tree regeneration.

By the end of the Neolithic and at the advent of the Bronze Age, c. 2000 B.C., humans began to settle into the landscape on permanent farms, while maintaining their hunting activities, including the long, slow process of reducing predators. Their farms were on the best land, above the flooding and on the low ridges and gentle slopes of the valley floor below the 700-foot contour. Because of later activity these are very hard to find archaeologically, but we can readily see where they buried their dead, usually cremated, under cairns built of loose stones on the mountain crests (Figs. 15 & 16).

Fig. 15: Carn Fflur, a round cairn which is part of a large cairn-field on a ridge to the south of Strata Florida.

One very notable exception to this pattern of hill-top location lies close to Strata Florida itself at the source (blaen) of the Afon Glasffrwd (Fig. 16). Here there is a cluster of monuments lying in a hollow almost completely encircled by hills. This hollow once contained a small lake, now in-filled with peat, as well as springs and a large flush of boggy ground.

Fig. 16: The context of the monument group at Blaenglasffrwd.

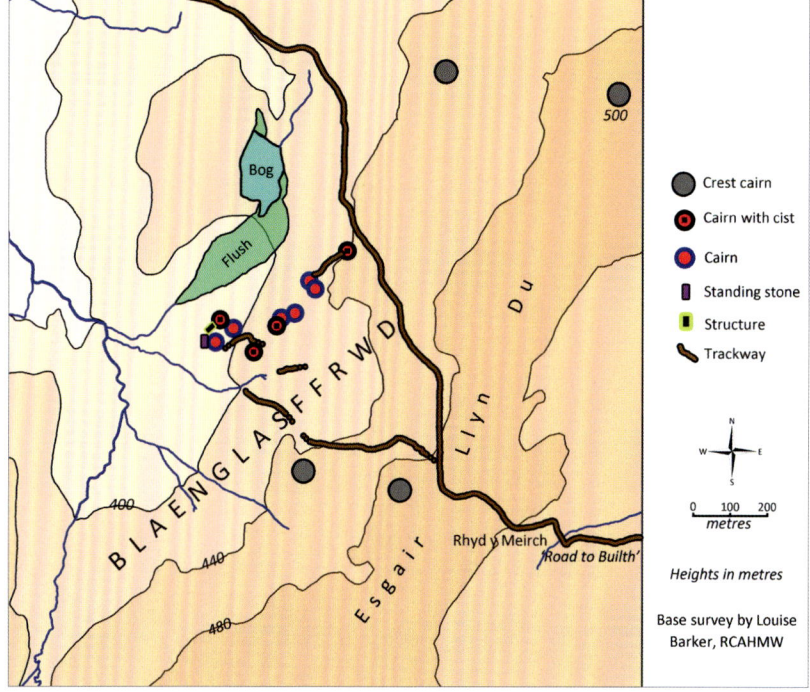

There are at least ten large cairns in the group, accompanied by a small row of upright stones, a rectangular structure and a series of narrow paths between the monuments, one leading down to a spring (Fig. 17). This exceptional group was probably created as a site of ritual related to the celebration and worship of water or its deities.

Fig. 17: A large Bronze Age burial cairn with central cist, at Blaenglasffrwd.

Within the Strata Florida region at this date there are also traces of enigmatic 'burnt mounds' which, on excavation, in addition to multitudes of burnt stones and remains of fire, often have large wooden troughs at their centres made from hollowed tree-trunks. Their distribution tends to be around the fringes of Cors Caron (Fig. 18) and they are variously interpreted as places for the exploitation of aquatic life and/or locations for feasting and other ritual performances.

Throughout the Bronze Age (2000-700 B.C.) and into the Iron Age (700 B.C. to A.D. 70), the landscape filled with settlement, until all was under some form of agriculture whether cultivation or grazing on the *ffridd* and *mynydd*. We can conclude from the distribution and siting of hill-forts (Fig. 18) such as Pen-y-bannau (Fig. 3), that there were also complex social formations and hierarchies at a variety of levels from regional tribes to more localised communities within which kin-based networks conducted the farming on a daily basis. It is difficult to know exactly how this worked, but we can look to later Welsh and Irish law codes to get some inkling that rights of access and inheritance governed how land was held and transmitted, while obligations of labour and tribute in kind maintained the controlling warrior and priestly elites. Great embanked enclosures (the 'hill-forts') came to dominate the sky-lines and local tribes and communities were engaged in the long-term struggle to control resources and keep safe.

Fig. 18: Distribution of known prehistoric sites within the Upper Teifi environs area. Also added to the map are the boundaries of historic parishes and reconstructed boundaries (in red) of the pre- Norman period. This gives a strong indication that the hill-forts especially can be directly related to the territories of ancient communities.

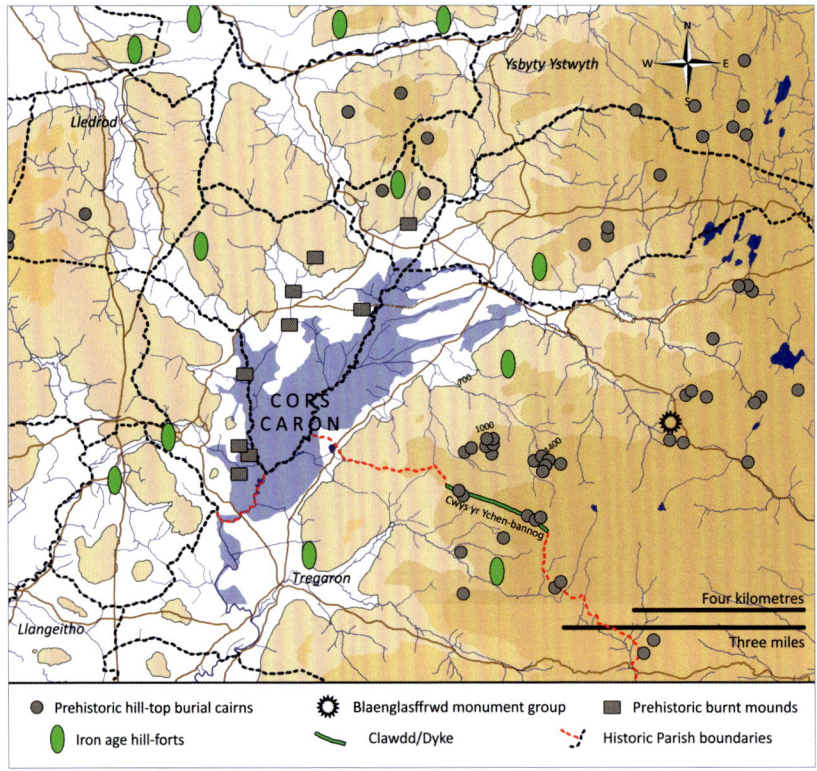

One strange object has come down to us from the very end of the Iron Age: a small stylised human figure which was discovered in a peat bog near Strata Florida about 1900 (Fig. 19). It is made of box-wood and stands only 12.9 cm. high, recently radio-carbon dated to 43 B.C.-A.D. 67, and it may be a votive offering ritually cast into the bog and associated with fertility in some way.

Fig. 19: A small box-wood figurine recovered from a bog at Strata Florida, possibly the one now within Coed-y-bont at the western end of the abbey precinct.

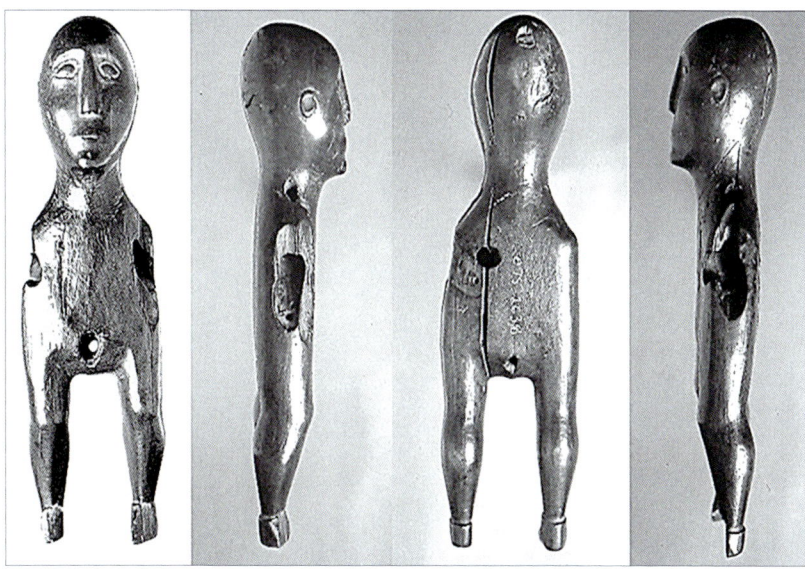

Fig. 20: The line of the Roman road (Sarn Helen) crossing the Cambrian Mountains some miles to the south of Strata Florida in Cellan.

Into this landscape, c. A.D. 80, came the Romans who, for a short while, drove military roads such as Sarn Helen (Fig. 20) across the Welsh uplands, linked and defended by forts, which at least nominally brought the local tribes within the empire. Their main target, however, seems to have been the rich mineral lodes to be found in the Cambrian Mountains and not the creation of agricultural estates and towns as they did in lowland Britain. Their interest seems to have lasted only until the mid-second century A.D., with most of their forts abandoned or only intermittently used until the final Roman withdrawal from Britannia at the beginning of the fifth century. It was the Romans who first introduced Christianity into the social landscapes of Wales, but we are unsure whether, if at all, it established itself in the Strata Florida region.

It is not really until the fifth or sixth centuries that Christianity began to embed itself in local communities and its rituals became accepted as the core relationship with the sacred. The abundant texts of the Lives of the Saints give the core narratives, but we also have sculptured and inscribed stones, dated from the sixth to early twelfth centuries, most of which are in churches and churchyards where, it is assumed, they were originally sited as memorials. There are also the churchyards themselves whose enclosures (place-name *llan*), together with related archaeological features, seem to identify them as belonging to this early period.

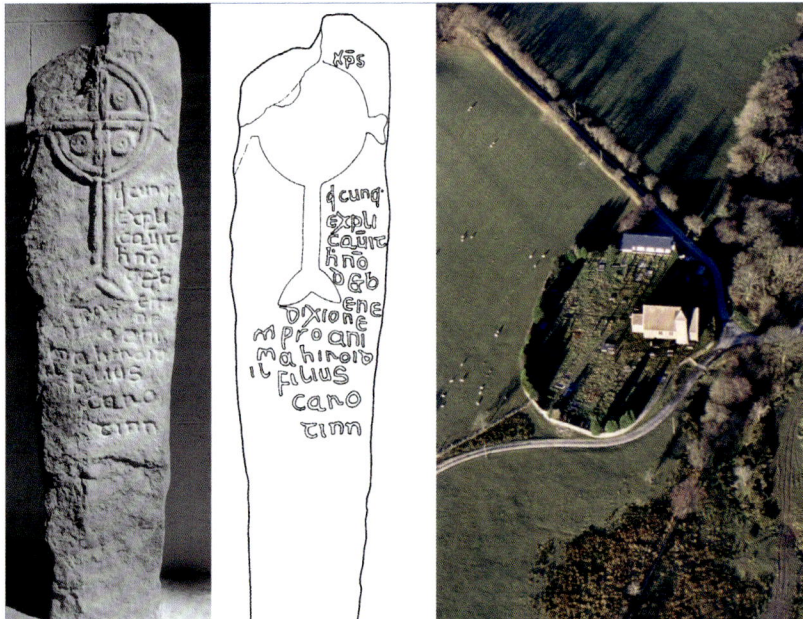

Fig. 21: Llanwnnws church and Dark Age monument. The church lies in its early monastic enclosure some three miles to the north-west of Strata Florida. The ninth-century monument, today standing in the church porch, commemorates a man of Irish descent, Hiroidil, son of Carotinn.

Virtually no documents survive to tell us in any detail how this 'Celtic Church' was organised on the ground. However, we do know that territories ('lands') were run by central monasteries or *clasau*, also sometimes called 'mother churches', with lay monks in communities run on an almost tribal basis by secular abbots. In these territories local pastoral and spiritual care was administered by monks from the central monastery in small chapels or cells constructed within community graveyard enclosures as in the case of Llanwnnws ('the enclosure of St Gwnnws': Fig. 21 and no. 6 on Fig. 22). In the Strata Florida region spread either side of the Cambrian Mountains, we are able to plot not just these distinctive enclosure sites, but the lands of at least two of the central monasteries of St Padarn at Llanbadarn Fawr and of St David at Llanddewi Brefi (Fig. 22).

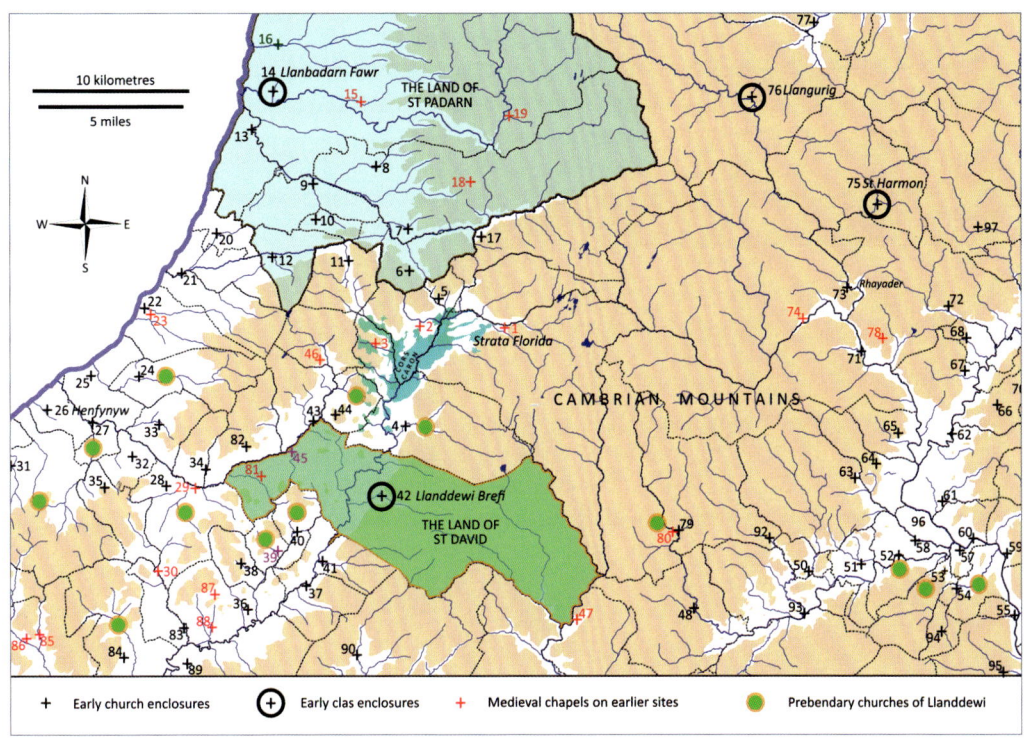

Fig. 22: The distribution of early church enclosure sites within the bounds of the parishes of which they later became the centre. The map also shows the likely limits of the 'lands' of the clas monasteries at Llanddewi Brefi and at Llanbadarn Fawr. These are mapped from evidence in later medieval documents, with the full extent of the 'Land of St David' suggested also by the prebendary churches attached to Llanddewi in the later Middle Ages.

This regional system (Fig. 22) was gradually swept away in a major ecclesiastical reform which was accelerated in the wake of the early Norman Conquest in partial fulfilment of an undertaking made to Pope Alexander II by William I in return for his support of the invasion. The vow was, in general, to establish the Pope's authority over the church, including Wales which was only nominally under the arch-diocese of Canterbury. Here the authority of Rome was only weakly followed with many of the old practices maintained.

It was only in the early 12th century, however, that the Welsh church was brought fully into line with European practice with four dioceses, Llandaff, Bangor, St Asaph's and St David's, albeit all centred at former major *clas* locations. The local church was reorganised into regular parishes under diocesan control, although the actual location of religious practice was largely not changed. Stone churches for the conduct of the Catholic liturgy were slowly added into the enclosures of the Celtic antecedents, perhaps replacing timber chapels. This local change took time and was still in progress when the Cistercians of Strata Florida were injected into the religious and spiritual chemistry of the region. These came as one aspect of reformed monasticism which, along with other orders, replaced the Welsh concepts of the monastery with more European ideas of contemplative communities, serving God separate from the worldly responsibilities for pastoral administration.

This transitional event for the Christian faith in Wales was to leave a long-term legacy in the sentiment of the people who live here. It is clear that the Welsh way of doing things was not entirely lost in the new order. We have already seen that the old centres were retained, albeit with new architectures, and people's journeys to worship probably remained the same. Secular society and patterns of life also remained largely unchanged in the countryside. In the early middle ages laws had been codified and procedures about such things as crime, inheritance and render of goods to the elites had all been adjusted, more in line with some of the law codes of England or Carolingian Europe. In essence, however, they retained a strong element of tribal and kin power within them.

The political context for all this was the shadowy emergence, in the post-Roman world, of a series of often-competing political territories or polities. In this world the leaders of the elites, the Princes, vied for authority, cementing together, from time to time and usually only for the lifetimes of strong individuals, confederacies and more extensive areas of dominance. Although never completely stable in terms of their boundaries due to persistent attempts to extend territory, it is clear that key entities were consolidated by the seventh and eighth centuries. These then persisted as more or less settled concepts of identity and how Wales should be constructed in terms of secular power. By the eleventh century south-western Wales centred around the concept of Deheubarth, a shifting conglomeration of three distinct units: Dyfed (now mainly Pembrokeshire), Ystrad Tywi (north Carmarthenshire) and Ceredigion. It was this concept which motivated the lifetime actions of the Lord Rhys ap Gruffudd, who became its prince in 1155.

Designing Strata Florida into the landscape

Fig. 23: Robert FitzStephen illustrated in an Irish manuscript.

The history of Wales for this period can be bewildering for the first-time reader, and its complexity was compounded in the twelfth century by the addition of Anglo-Normans, sanctioned to intrude into and claim territory by the laws of the March. Thus, in the case of Strata Florida, the abbey was first founded in 1164 and, according to a Papal list, its first benefactor was an Anglo-Norman, Robert FitzStephen (Fig. 23).

In his own person Robert reflected the complexity of the twelfth century. He was a Norman knight, but one with a royal Welsh mother, Nest, herself daughter of the last King of Dyfed, Rhys ap Tewdwr, while his father Stephen was custodian of the Norman castle of Cardigan, a post to which he succeeded. Robert's grant was made, as was the way with the Cistercians, to a mother house, in this case Whitland, which then sent out 12 monks to create its daughter monastery at Strata Florida. Whitland itself had been founded at some point before 1145 by Bernard, the first Norman Bishop of St David's, while its own mother-house was Clairvaux, founded in 1115 by one of the Cistercian order's main driving spirits and ideologues, St Bernard (Fig. 24).

Fig. 24: Tonsured head, from a full-length figure, of a monk about half life-size found in one of the transept chapels at Strata Florida during the nineteenth-century excavations. It is believed to represent St. Bernard of Clairvaux, the founding house of the Whitland family of Cistercian monasteries in Wales.

One text of c. 1180, however, a history of the foundation of Vaucelles Abbey in northern France, itself a daughter house of Clairvaux, also laid claim to have had a role in founding both Whitland and Strata Florida. Both Cynan abbot of Whitland in 1164 and Enoc the founding abbot of Strata Florida were Welshmen trained at Vaucelles. If this history is to be given any credence, Enoc attracted 30 choir monks and 40 lay brothers to Strata Florida within four years of the foundation.

By 1165 Robert FitzStephen was out of office, imprisoned by Rhys ap Gruffudd, Prince of Deheubarth, after he had captured Cardigan Castle. The year before, Rhys had also taken Ceredigion from Richard de Clare, the Earl of Hertford. There is embedded in this history, however, a conundrum in the accepted account of the founding of Strata Florida. If, as the Vatican document asserts, the first grant was made in 1164 by Robert FitzStephen, it must be reconciled with the knowledge that he actually had no authority to give away land that was either in the hands of Richard de Clare or newly held by Lord Rhys. The only other evidence we have is at one remove: in 1285 Edward I's officials inspected documents relating back to a grant by Lord Rhys to the monks of Strata Florida of a block of land around Cors Caron. When exactly Rhys gave this first grant is not recorded, but it was prior to 1182-3 at the latest, and it may be that it was intended as a confirmation by Rhys of Robert's grant. Edward I's inspection, however, has no mention of the Castellan of Cardigan and the wording of the document simply records Lord Rhys as the benefactor. It may be that Rhys was both the secular founder of Strata Florida in 1164 and its re-founder in 1184.

Even if Robert FitzStephen did make the first grant, it was Lord Rhys who was its major patron almost from the start. This was how he was regarded by an undated bull or edict of Pope Alexander III (1159-81) which ensured the abbey lay outside of diocesan control. In all, however, the new institution was a clear departure from the monasticism of the *clas*. It was no longer in the hands of local elite secular kindreds with hereditary bishops and abbots, but there is a question still to be asked about how much of a change this all was.

We can begin by asking also — why here? In the answer to this question may lie the clues to understanding what actually was built in terms of plan and architecture, and how it stood as an institution in the world of Wales. The first grant of land was modest as far as we can tell, but this does have elements of guesswork about it (Fig. 25).

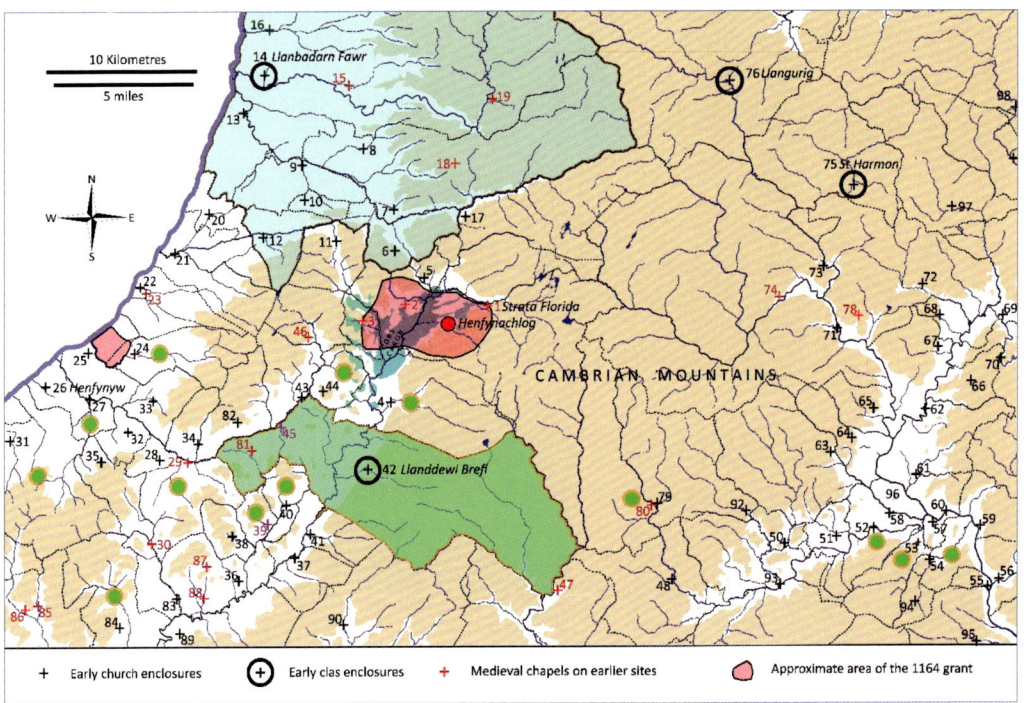

Fig. 25: The approximate area of the first grant of 1164 as recorded in 1285.

One of the difficulties in plotting names from the charter onto a modern map is that only some of the names can be readily identified with places to be found in later documents. In trying to identify the charter place-names there are essentially two different approaches. The first is etymological, i.e. trying to reconstruct what the name might be in linguistic terms, and the other is to consider the coherence of the grant topographically and then look for possibilities, i.e. making the assumption that unidentified places are most likely to have been near places that can be identified. The maps produced here work on the second principle.

Whatever the limitations of trying to reconstruct the 1165 grant the generality is clear: the charter granted a small area of land around Aberarth on the coast of Cardigan Bay giving access to the sea, and a more substantial but separate inland farming block in the upper Teifi valley (Fig. 25). This unified coherent estate would have provided enough resources for the monks to sustain an abbey, and seems to have been founded on what many presume is its first location at Henfynachlog ('The Old Monastery'), alongside the stream, Afon Fflur, from which the abbey is thought to have taken its name. This was first reported by the man who ran the archaeological excavations at Strata Florida in 1887-90, Stephen Williams. Unfortunately the current project has been unable to detect it on the site marked on the 1886 Ordnance Survey map (Fig. 26) and we shall have to search elsewhere.

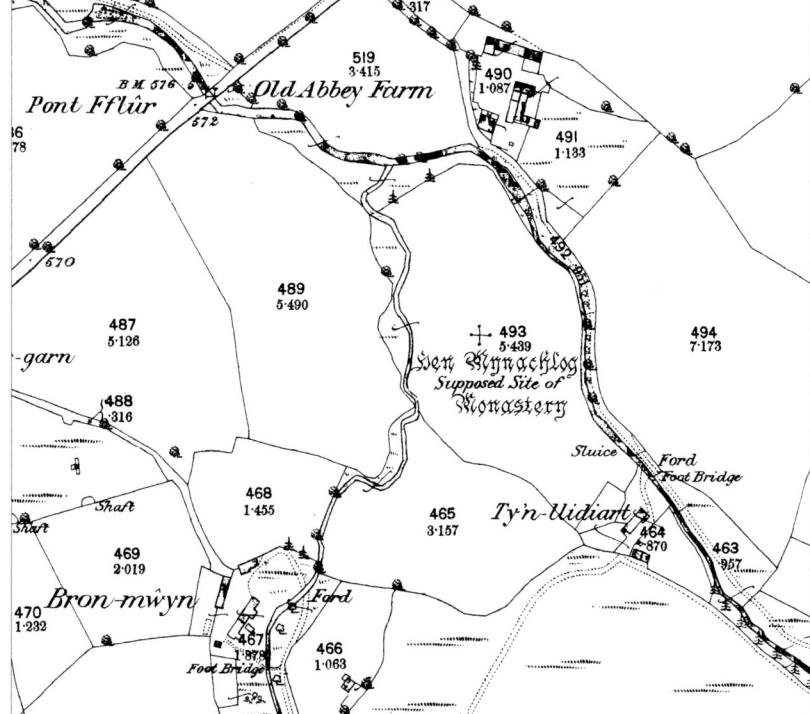

Fig. 26: The site of Henfynachlog marked on the first edition Ordnance Survey 1:2500 map surveyed in 1886 and published in 1889. Geophysics in the field marked have failed to show any clear signs of the stone building foundations reported by Stephen Williams.

The evidence that there was an earlier site for Strata Florida is usually thought to be the annal for 1201 in the Brut y Tywysogion:

> In that year the community of Strata Florida went to the new church on the eve of Whit Sunday, after it had been nobly and handsomely built.

This change of location appears to be part of a major change in the political and cultural intention of Strata Florida. Although supported and endowed by Lord Rhys from the start of his rule in Ceredigion, the political sands had further shifted in his favour when he gave the abbey a huge grant eclipsing the earlier one. By 1184 when he made this grant, Rhys had become an official of the English crown while retaining all his own sovereignty as Prince of relatively stable Deheubarth.

Rhys had, in 1171, reached an agreement with Henry II undertaking not to attack the forces of the king and accepting he was Henry's feudal vassal. For this Rhys was confirmed in the possession of all his territories and made Chief Justice of the crown in 'all of Deheubarth' which gave him jurisdiction over all the Welsh princes of the south. This position brought immense authority, but its ambivalence also contained the seeds of its own destruction: it ultimately became impossible to ride two such strong and wilful horses. Rhys was now at the height of his powers. Since 1146 he had been engaged, with his brothers and half-brothers, on the more or less continuous project, begun by his father, Gruffudd ap Rhys, of attempting to get permanent control over Deheubarth in south-western and central Wales.

By 1171 Rhys must have begun to believe that this project was well on the way to being achieved, backed as he was by the strongest secular kingdom in Western Europe. He held the first Eisteddfod in Cardigan in 1176, celebrating Welsh culture. He built stone castles, founded two religious houses at Talley and Llanllŷr, and supported two others at Whitland and Strata Florida. In other words he behaved as, and adopted the posture of, a feudal monarch. What was missing were the operational capacities of a state with its systems of command and exaction and a bureaucracy to administer it all. Without this Deheubarth and the other Welsh princedoms (Pura Wallia as it was known) were little more than a series of shifting and uncertain confederacies with occasional overall dominance exerted over neighbours. With an established state, however, succession of governance and its institutions was guaranteed, whatever king was in power. In the twelfth century that bureaucratic and administrative experience which maintained the Angevin state was centralised and vested largely in the literate priesthood and its senior clergy. To secure his position as a monarch among those of Europe Rhys would have needed a Westminster Abbey, as Henry II had, staffed with clerks in the service of the state working to create and sustain a complex series of centralised functions. When he founded Strata Florida was it his intention to do this?

There is little written evidence to suggest that he had such matters on his mind. However, in the preamble to the grant of 1184, effectively re-founding Strata Florida, he called himself 'Prince of South Wales' and in two other sources he used the title 'Prince of Wales' (or 'Prince of the Welsh'). This concept was better and more consistently articulated by Llywelyn ap Iorwerth, Prince of Gwynedd, a generation later. To speculate further about his motivation and intentions all we can do today is look at Rhys's creative actions and, as in the case of Strata Florida, at the material survival and ask why it came to be where it was. In other words how did it come to be a European institution with a transcendent and abiding Welsh identity?

We can begin by exploring the act of giving in 1184 when Rhys stood in front of his army, with all his senior people and his family about him, at St Brigid's church, on the west bank of the River Wye opposite Rhayader and signed the charter effectively re-founding Strata Florida. The words of the charter of 1184 may contain clues to Rhys's intentions. First it was very much more substantial than 1164, albeit in structure basically the same, with an inland core and a coastal component. Next, it was executed not in his Princedom of Deheubarth, but in Cantref Deuddwr, a largely upland terrain to the west of the river Wye and of uncertain and contested status for much of its history. He would have been acting here as Chief Justiciar for the English crown and as the dominant Welsh leader of his generation within Pura Wallia (Fig. 27).

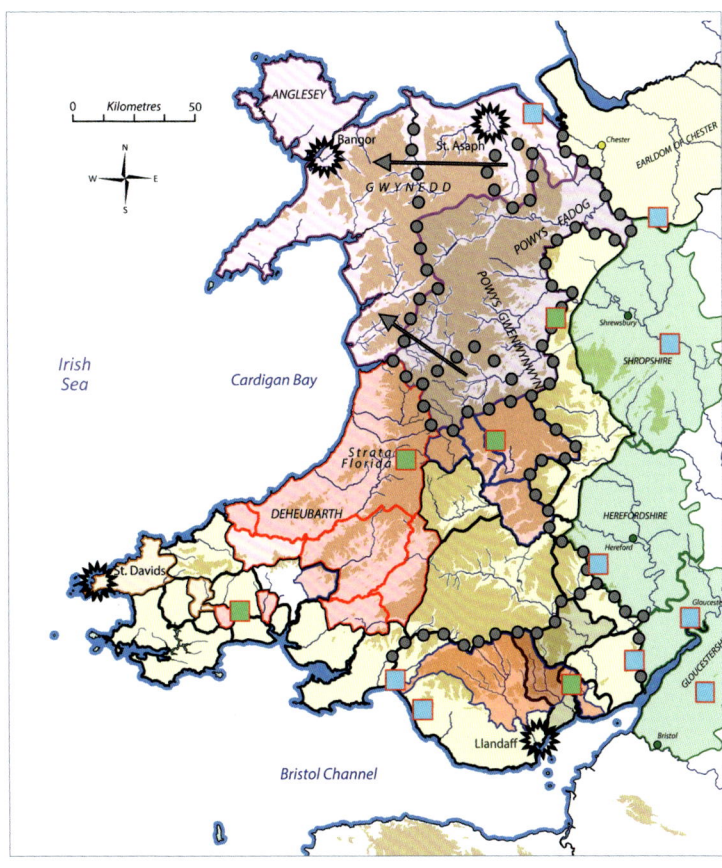

Fig. 27: The disposition of territories and authority in 1184 set within the new Anglo-Norman diocesan structures.

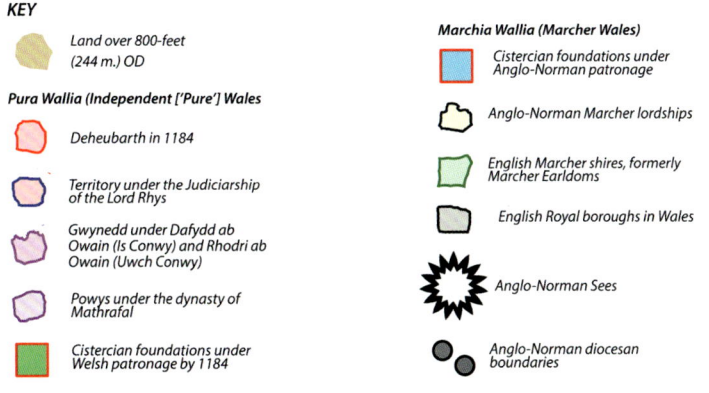

KEY

Land over 800-feet (244 m.) OD

Pura Wallia (Independent ['Pure'] Wales)

Deheubarth in 1184

Territory under the Judiciarship of the Lord Rhys

Gwynedd under Dafydd ab Owain (Is Conwy) and Rhodri ab Owain (Uwch Conwy)

Powys under the dynasty of Mathrafal

Cistercian foundations under Welsh patronage by 1184

Marchia Wallia (Marcher Wales)

Cistercian foundations under Anglo-Norman patronage

Anglo-Norman Marcher lordships

English Marcher shires, formerly Marcher Earldoms

English Royal boroughs in Wales

Anglo-Norman Sees

Anglo-Norman diocesan boundaries

Finally, the grant was made to the Cistercian order. Before Rhys's accommodation with Henry II in 1171, a few Cistercian houses had been created by the Anglo-Normans of the eastern and southern Marches (Fig. 27). In only two cases were there foundations in Pura Wallia proper, at Strata Florida itself and Strata Marcella in 1170 by Owain Cyfeiliog, Prince of Powys. Post-1171, came Cwm-hir in 1176 founded by Cadwallon ap Madog of Maelienydd, then Llantarnam in 1179 under the patronage of Hywel ab Iorwerth of Caerleon, and then Aberconwy in 1186 founded by princes of Gwynedd. Then, in the following decades came two Cistercian nunneries at Llanllŷr in Ceredigion (Lord Rhys, pre-1197) and Llanllugan in Cedewain, Powys (Maredudd ap Rhobert, c. 1190). Finally, shortly after Rhys's death in 1197, Cymer was founded by Gruffudd ap Cynan, prince of Gwynedd and his brother Maredudd ap Cynan lord of Meirionydd, c.1198, as well as Valle Crucis in 1201 by Madog ap Gruffudd Maelor, lord of Iâl in Northern Powys.

All of these foundations were daughters or grand-daughters, the 'family', of Whitland, itself by then being strongly supported by Lord Rhys and it is possible to think that the adoption of the Cistercians as the monastic order of choice by Welsh princes might have been strategic. In the midst of this too, the Lord Rhys made his massive land grant to Strata Florida and the process of building on a new site had begun. Its central place in Wales and its ambitious nature suggests strongly also that it was conceived as a lynch-pin of this strategy, but why the Cistercians? There are, perhaps, three reasons. First, their ascetic conduct of the Rule of St Benedict resonated with the Celtic practices and miraculous self-sacrifices to be read about in the Saints' Lives. Second, the order answered to the Popes in Rome and were independent of the diocesan structure which, in Wales, owed its ultimate allegiance to Canterbury and the Anglo-Norman hierarchy. Finally, it had, as far as we can tell, a large Welsh element among its abbots and monks. Again, therefore, we can see Rhys falling into line with the wider European world, but retaining a sentiment for the older ways, avoiding, where he could, the direct control of Anglo-Norman kings and their intermediaries.

One other dimension to this is also worth noting. When the bishoprics of Wales were regularised, they were distributed at the four corners of the nation with nothing in the centre (Fig. 27). Notably there were sees in the princedoms of Powys and Gwynedd but none in Deheubarth. Medieval sees and their dioceses were an important element of the administrative structures of the feudal state, and the Lord Rhys had nothing to lean on in that respect. It is noticeable, therefore, that the Lord Rhys backed Strata Florida which seems to have been regarded as a successor to the earlier bishop-house of Llanbadarn. He also founded Talley Abbey close to, and perhaps also a successor to, the other main bishop-house of Deheubarth, at Llandeilo. This was actually Premonstratensian, although there were unsuccessful attempts in Rhys's lifetime to change its affiliation to Cistercian.

What, then, was given at St Brigid's church in 1184 and what can we infer from this about Lord Rhys's intentions? The size of the grant is impressive, spread as it is across the centre of Wales, straddling both sides of the Cambrian Mountains (Fig. 28). It covered a large tract of country, a great deal of it the open moorland of the Central Cambrian Mountains which would have functioned as mountain commons at the time of the grant. However, it also included good farming land on the valley slopes and floors of the upper Teifi, Aeron, Tywi, Elan and Wye rivers. Significantly too, nearly the whole of Cors Caron was given, a major resource at that time for peat, grazing, fishing and wild-fowling. Within the charter also the coastal holding of 1164 was expanded by three small grants.

We can first see that the core grant of 1184 seems to have been carefully placed between the former lands of St Padarn and St David as shown on Figs. 22 and 28. In part this is because the St Padarn territory had been granted in 1111 by Gilbert de Clare to the monastery of St Peter in Gloucester and technically was not within Rhys's power to give. However, Llanbadarn seems to have continued to function as a *clas* church in the old way well into the later twelfth century if not beyond. In the case of St David a large core was retained by the reformed see as its own manor. Beyond this the parish priests of former constituents of the wider *clas* territory were given prebendary status, thus continuing to serve at Llanddewi, as at St Padarn, in a college of canons. Both churches when rebuilt in this period continued to reflect their ancient status with large cruciform structures containing extended presbyteries to house the multiple priesthood.

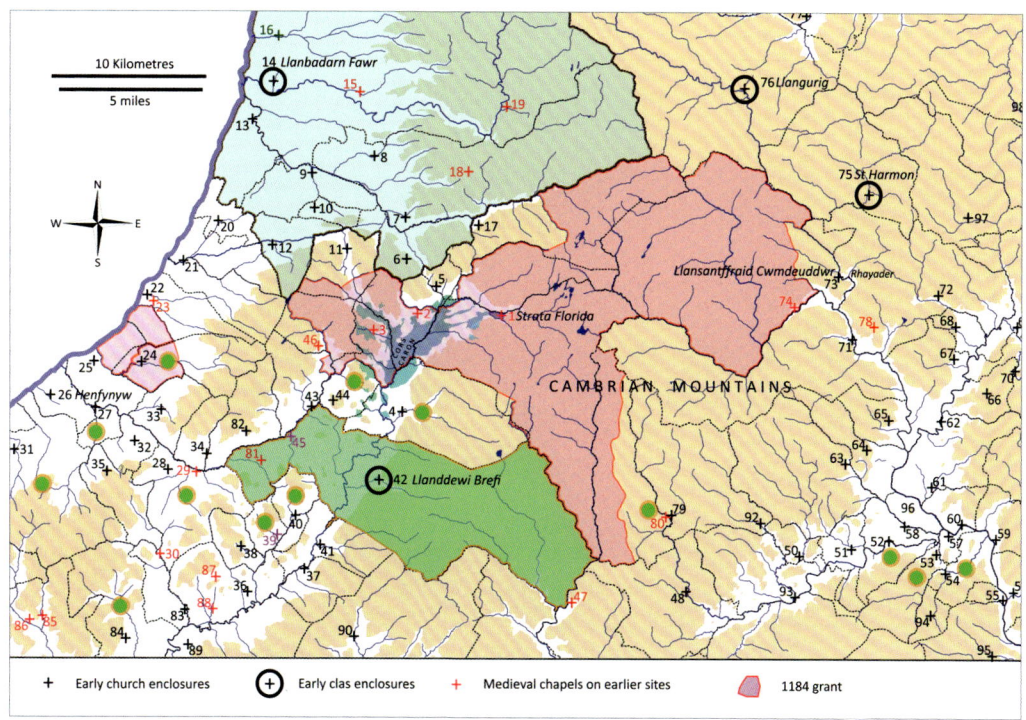

Fig. 28: Lands granted by Lord Rhys ap Gruffudd in 1184 when re-founding Strata Florida Abbey.

Another important element of this is the relationship to the new diocesan parochial system, something we can explore through the map evidence, especially if we focus a little more narrowly on the western end of the core grant (Fig. 29).

Fig. 29: The grant of 1184 with the consequent rearrangement of the parishes in the upper Teifi valley. This shows the proposed area of a reconstructed early parish, which we are giving the provisional title of 'Ystrad Fflur'.

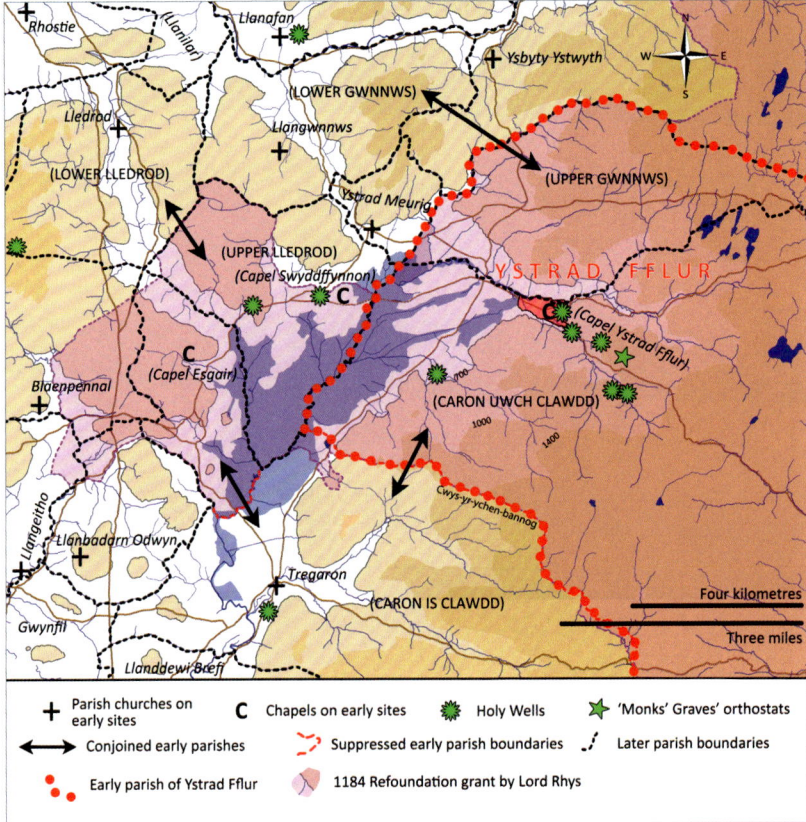

In the period leading up to the 1184 grant, the process of parochial reorganisation in the diocese of St David's had probably begun during the episcopacy of Bernard (1117-1145), the first Anglo-Norman bishop. This had involved using the network of early sites of the *clas* system with their cemetery enclosures, such as Llangwnnws (Fig. 21) and redesignating them as the centres of fixed parishes under diocesan control. We can also see that, in creating the parish areas they adopted the territories or pastoral communities of these early smaller sites, and we can think of these as 'early parishes'. When the 1184 grant was given, however, we can identify that three of these early sites were not made into parish centres, but left rather as chapels attached to adjacent parishes. Two of these are Swyddffynnon attached to Lledrod and Capel Esgair attached to Tregaron (Caron). The third is Strata Florida itself, now the church of St Mary's, rebuilt in 1815, but in this case, its original early parish seems to have been split two ways: the northern part was made into a detached portion of Llangwnnws parish, Upper Gwnnws, and the southern into a township of Caron (Tregaron), Caron-uwch-clawdd.

Two key things emerge from all this which are important to our understanding of how Strata Florida came to be created. First, when the grant was given an agreement must have been negotiated with the diocese of St. David's so that the abbey, within its granted area, had no parish churches in its jurisdiction, in other words it had no 'appropriated churches', something which the Cistercian order expressly forbad. Next, that the early Christian site of Strata Florida, the chapel and its cemetery, prior to 1184, was originally at the centre of a very large early parish (we have provisionally called 'Ystrad Fflur') which stretched over the watershed eastwards to the Afon Tywi with, on its southern boundary, the early medieval dyke of Cwys-yr-ychen-bannog. As such it bears comparison with the core parishes of both Llanddewi Brefi and Llanbadarn.

This designing of the Strata Florida core grant into the landscape may tell us several things. Care was taken not to upset the Anglo-Norman and papal project of reform and this probably involved a deal of negotiation before the charter was drawn up and signed at Rhayader. Care was also being taken, it would seem, to reflect a strongly prevailing sentiment for the old ways, the familiar Welsh patterns of spirituality and worship, and for preserving them in some form as a clear act of syncretism. There is also a possibility that the space between St Padarn and St David was an ancient one and may once have been filled by another *clas* with its territory centred on Strata Florida itself.

Designing the abbey into its setting: an early site?

To consider the grounds for making such a suggestion we have to work with some fairly circumstantial evidence which emerges from a few key features in and around the abbey of Strata Florida as it survives to us today. The present site was the result of a conscious re-location, something which is not unknown in the placing of Cistercian monasteries.

Sometimes the siting was simply more favourable and in the case of Strata Florida this was certainly a factor, since the old site would not have easily accommodated the size of the re-founded abbey precinct. However, another motivation also played its part. There is now a realisation that a body of reformed monasteries were deliberately built on the sites of pre-Norman houses, perhaps even of *clas* status. This was relatively common in Wales as in the cases of at least two other Cistercian houses at Llanllŷr and Margam, and eleven others housing both Augustinian canons and Benedictine monks.

There is also some detailed archaeological and map evidence to suggest that this re-location to an earlier site was actually carried out in a carefully designed and crafted manner. We can begin by postulating and mapping the approximate location of a pre-Cistercian monastery (Fig. 30).

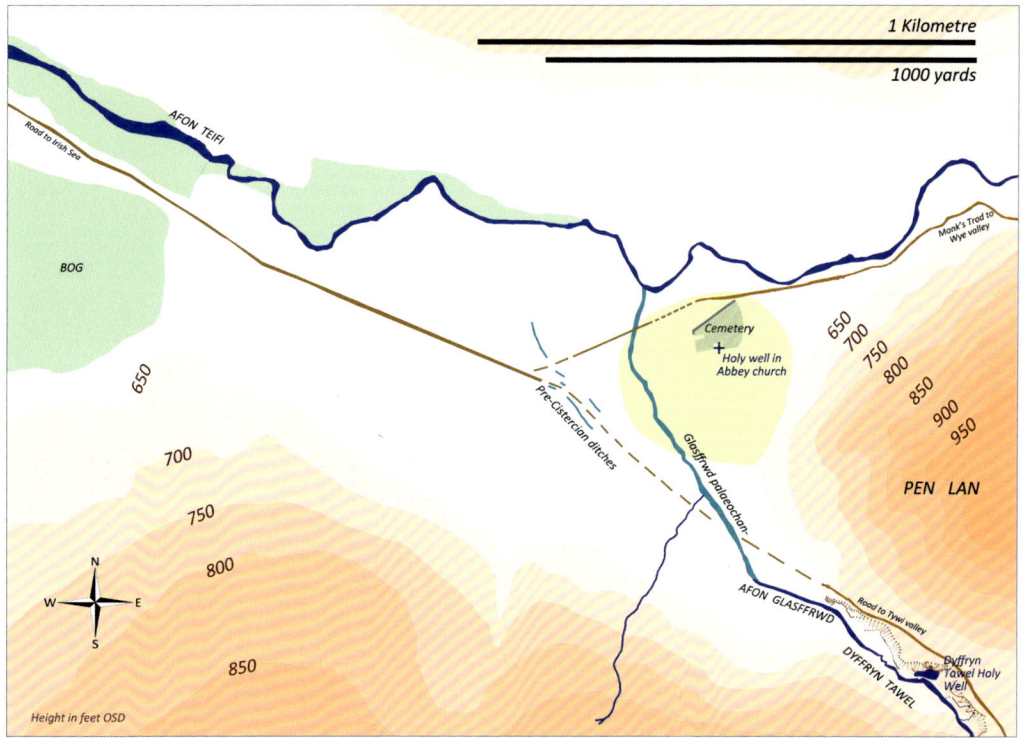

Fig. 30: Speculative plan of a pre-Cistercian monastery with OSD height in feet.

We are able to reconstruct the line of the two ancient routeways coming over the Cambrian Mountains from the east as they pass the site, converging at a point to the west of the present farm. The route then runs westwards as the Lôn Lacs, towards the coast at Aberarth. In the angle between the two there is still today the parochial cemetery from which a ninth-century burial with a carved slab over it was recovered in 1847 (Fig. 31). Two earthen banks to north and west, to be seen within the enlarged modern graveyard, seem to define an earlier cemetery enclosure. Within the cemetery today is the former parish church of St Mary's which originally was a medieval chapel. In 1546 a petition to the post-dissolution crown administrators stated that it held services for the lay parishioners of the area and was served by the monks of Strata Florida. That a lay cemetery and chapel was included within the precinct of the abbey so close to the abbey church is unusual. Such cemeteries, however, were an integral part of the layout of early monasteries of the Celtic Church and often lay at their core. The retention of this burial ground at Strata Florida is, of itself, an indicator of how the Cistercians were planning their monastery both within the requirements of reformed monasticism and respecting key elements of an older tradition.

Fig. 31: A ninth-century cross-inscribed stone today standing upright at the east end of St Mary's church. It was originally lying recumbent within the cemetery immediately to the east of the church. It has been suggested that the five holes, drilled to a depth of c. 10cm., were intended to hold candles or tapers. Clearly this was a significant burial, but it is hard to know whether it was for a secular leader or a priest, perhaps even an early saint.

The position of the abbey church, as seen in air photographs (Fig. 32) may also suggest that it was laid out over the top of the southern part of the early cemetery.

Fig. 32: The position of the Cistercian church in relation to the early cemetery to the north. 'The position of the holy well at the crossing of the abbey church can be clearly seen to be on a different alignment (see Fig. 34).

The reason for this seems to have been to enable the master masons to lay the abbey church foundations around a pre-existing holy well contemporary with the early cemetery, so that it was positioned deliberately in front of the high altar (Fig. 33). The holy well itself was rebuilt by the abbey masons and plumbed into the monastery's water supply which itself originated at another holy well up the Glasffrwd valley to the south. When rebuilt, however, they maintained its original alignment which is due east-west while the abbey church was aligned to sunset on St David's Day, itself, perhaps, a veiled reference to the patron saint of Wales.

Fig. 33: The holy well at the crossing of the abbey church, looking north-east. It has two flights of steps down to a square cistern in the base with the openings of two stone-lined conduits, one from the south' bringing the water in and one to north for the out-flow. The eastern set of steps leads from the high altar (to the right), while the other to the nave. This suggests that the holy well was intended to be part of a ceremony with monks officiating.

The early nature of the well seems to have been confirmed by a preliminary geophysics survey of the abbey transepts and crossing area (Fig. 34).

While more work will need to be done to determine the exact nature of the earlier site beneath the Cistercian abbey, there is enough now to suggest strongly that there was an earlier religious establishment there and that elements of its buildings and other features were consciously designed and absorbed into the design of the Cistercian church and precinct. As such it might be a candidate for a *clas* monastery whose territory sat between Llanbadarn to the north and Llanddewi Brefi to the south (Fig. 28).

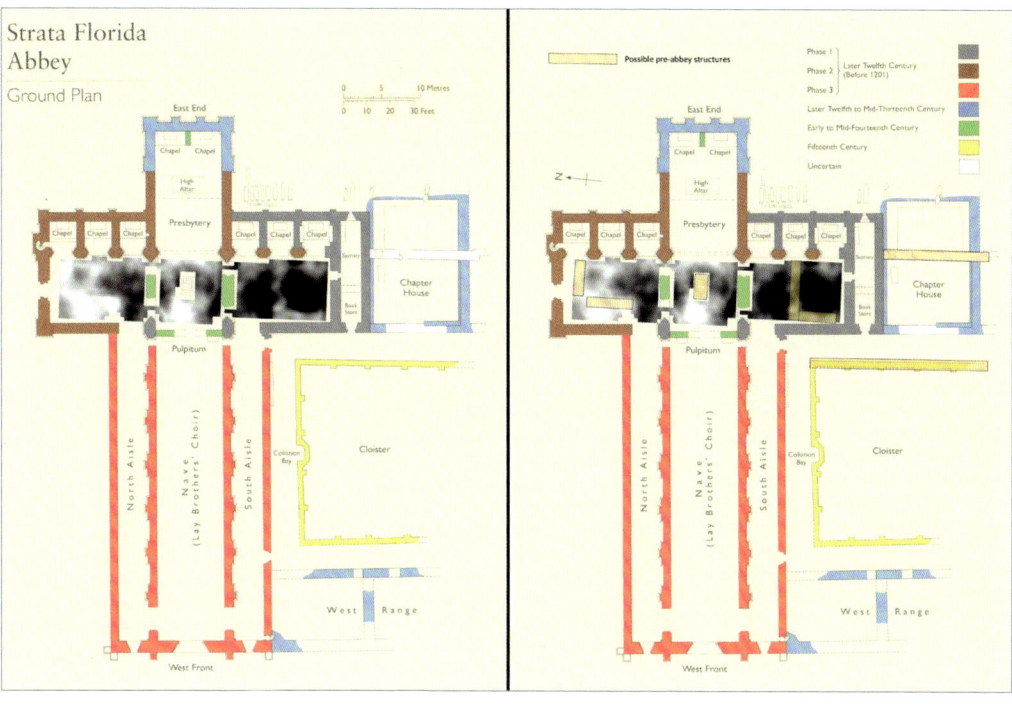

Fig. 34: Preliminary geophysics (resistivity) survey of the interior of the abbey church at the crossing and transepts. This appears to show the presence of earlier structures with the same alignment as the holy well. This includes the east wall of the cloister-garth and an otherwise unexplained early north-south wall dividing the chapter-house.

This resonates with a reference in a praise poem (*awdl*) by Guto'r Glyn to the abbey's fifteenth-century Abbot Rhys: in line 75 Strata Florida is called *Tai Gynfelyn* ('the houses of Cynfelyn'). This phraseology often refers to monasteries and Cynfelyn is a little-known saint of the seventh or eighth centuries whose name is also preserved at Llangynfelyn, Cwm Cynfelyn and Sarn Gynfelyn, all in north Ceredigion. Is the site beneath Strata Florida the monastery of Saint Cynfelyn?

Another element of the plan of Strata Florida which might be early are the carved grave-markers set at the heads of burial slabs lying outside the church in the angle between the Presbytery and the South Transept (Figs. 34 & 35). It is a matter of debate as to whether these stones are of the tenth or eleventh century and reused or were carved in a deliberately archaic form at the end of the twelfth century. If reused it is entirely possible that they were taken out of the early cemetery when the new abbey church was laid out.

Fig. 35: The burial markers in the re-entrant angle between the abbey church's presbytery and south transept. Several of the header stones are executed in a style pre-dating the abbey's foundation. The burials are in the most favoured location close to the high altar but external as Cistercian regulations required. They are, therefore, likely to be the first burials on the new site of the abbey and may be those of abbots or monks previously buried at Henfynachlog whose remains were moved when the new abbey was consecrated in 1201.

Although it is too soon to be certain about a monastery of St Cynfelyn, it is clear that the 1184 abbey was being planned and designed onto something that preceded it and now lies below today's monument. When we consider, however, the existence of this early site we need also to look for a moment at a wider landscape context. The holy well in the church at Strata Florida was not alone in this area. Our map of the Upper Teifi valley (Fig. 29) shows the locations of known holy wells and while they are quite liberally scattered through the landscape, the cluster in the Glasffrwd valley is distinctive. The holy well captured in the plan of the abbey is one of five currently identified within a short distance of each other (Fig. 36).

Fig. 36: The 'sacred valley' of the Afon Glasffrwd.

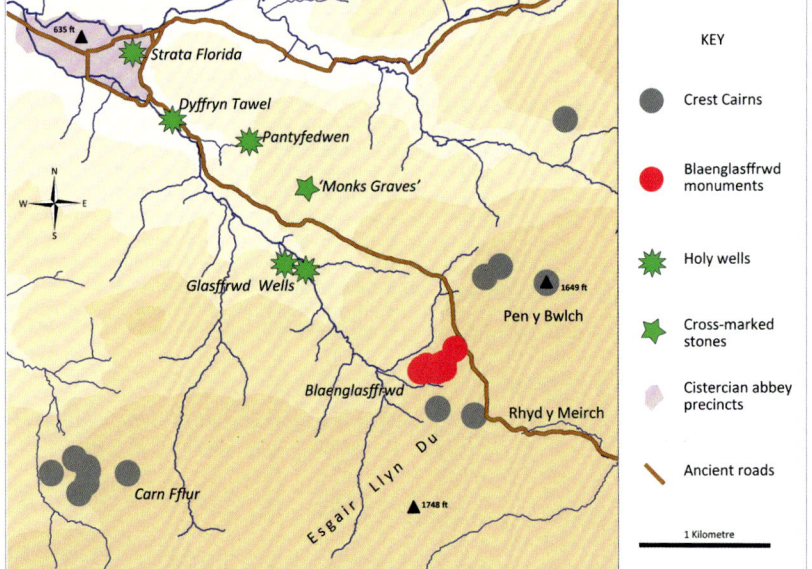

One is at the head of the water management system of the abbey and was created by quarrying back the rock face so that a spring issued into a small basin about three metres above the floor of the valley and then fell as a cascade into a pool at the head of a series of pools and leats (Fig. 37). Two flights of steps were also cut into the rock face so that the well was approached from above. This stretch of the Glasffrwd valley is called Dyffryn Tawel (the 'quiet valley').

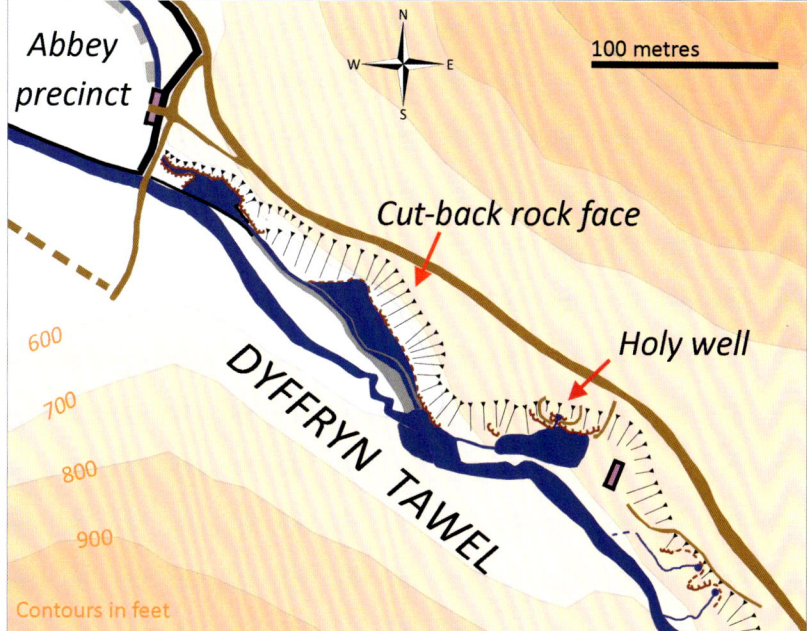

Fig. 37: Site of the Dyffryn Tawel holy well in relation to a plan reconstruction of the abbey's water management system at its point of origin.

A great deal of speculation has centred on this type of sacred site in the landscape: some are of considerable antiquity, for example the Coventina well on Hadrian's Wall which is Roman but dedicated to three local water deities. It is usually believed that these wells originate in a deep pagan past and are often associated in local folklore with healing and well-being. That deeper past is present in the Bronze Age monument cluster at Blaen-glasffrwd where water was the focus of veneration (Figs. 16 & 17). Are we seeing here the survival of a 'sacred valley' whose meanings to local society were simply reiterated down the centuries and where rituals of water persisted along the Afon Glasffrwd for thousands of years, from source to what became the heart of an abbey?

Designing the abbey into its setting: the new monastery

Including the holy well and the making of the water supply can be seen, therefore, as conscious acts of design in laying out the plan of the re-founded abbey, with intention of incorporating meaningful features of an earlier world.

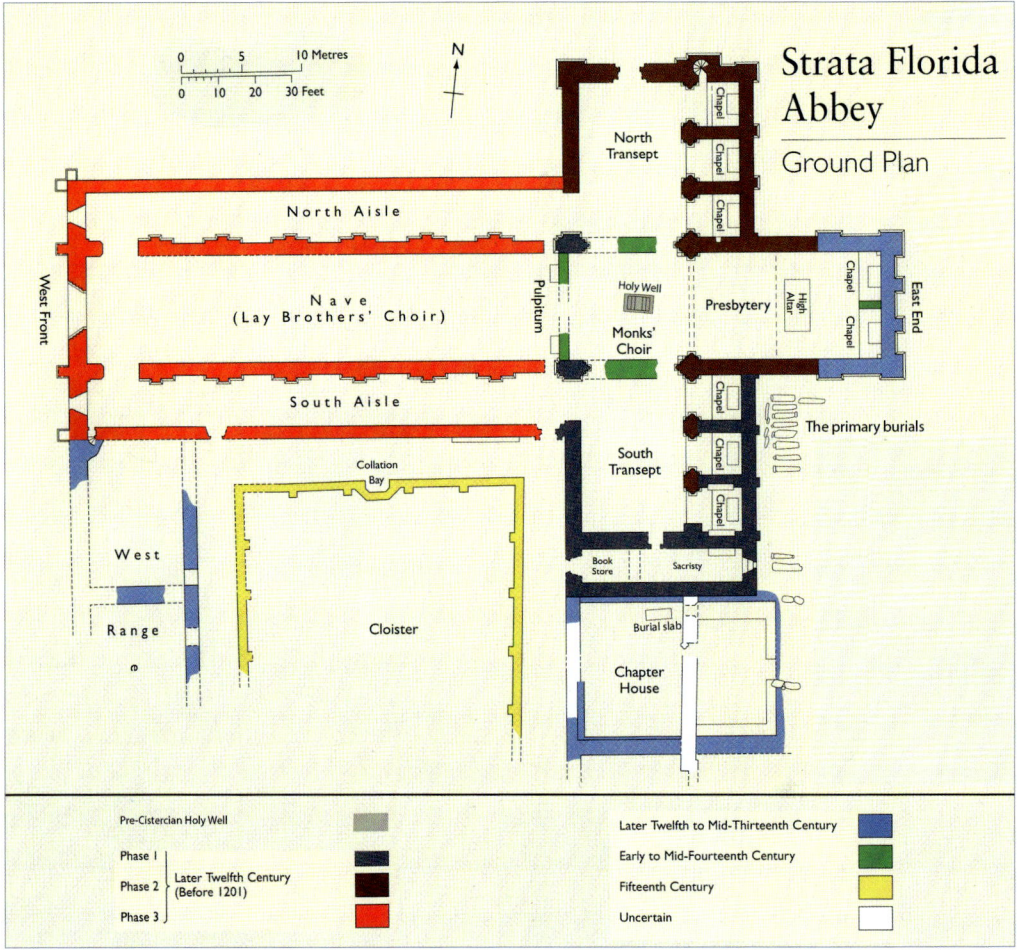

Fig. 38: Plan of the abbey remains within the Cadw monument. This plan shows the building sequences described by David Robinson in the Cadw guidebook, apart from the holy well dating added by David Austin.

On the other hand the building programme of the core buildings of the new abbey (Fig. 38) also created a church which, for the most part, was European in its architectural aspirations, but with one other significant nod to something earlier and more indigenous. Building was begun, as with all Cistercian monastic building, at the east end and the intention was to follow the 'Bernardine' plan as can be seen at Fontenay in Burgundy (Fig. 39).

Fig. 39: View of the east end of Fontenay Abbey in Burgundy. The church on the right shows the 'Bernardine' plan without a crossing tower.

As soon, however, as the presbytery, and transepts (each containing three chapels) had been completed, the decision was taken to have a church with a crossing tower in the English manner. Building then continued westwards with the church completed by 1201 as reported in the *Brut y Tywysogion*. The style of the architecture and its decorative features belong to the early Gothic period and it is striking how some of the carving has direct parallels with St David's cathedral. Building then continued into the cloister complex with the chapter house in the east range belonging stylistically to about 1220. Next came the south range which included the refectory, probably finished by 1250. It is likely that the west range was up shortly afterwards and the whole was topped off when the great bell was hung in 1255 in the crossing tower. The tiles of the nave floor were also laid at about the same time.

Within this building programme the masons did, however, incorporate a stylistic nod to an earlier period, to be found on the most impressive piece of surviving architecture at Strata Florida: the western portal (or doorway) of the church (Fig. 40). It is again, as with the well, a conscious absorption of tradition into the new order of doing things.

Fig. 40: The western portal of the abbey church executed in Dundry stone. It is stylistically Transitional between Early Gothic and Romanesque.

The portal in some senses sits comfortably in the canon of European architecture, transitional between Romanesque with its round-headed arch and the early Gothic with its five orders of roll and strap moulding. What is different, however, are the carved 'labels' or terminals which sit at the ends of the strap mouldings. There were once 15 carvings set symmetrically about the outer edge of the portal and of these four are gone or completely eroded (Fig. 40, 1, 2, 14 and 15). The rest, however, hark back to a much earlier style vocabulary, that of Celtic tradition in the manner of early medieval manuscripts and inscribed stones. Placing these at the entrance of the church, literally in a liminal position in the sacred geography of the architecture and the place, calls for close consideration. Four principal motifs can be seen (Fig. 41): roundels of 'tetraskele' with four interlocked spiral-arms (nos. 4, 5, 6, 7, 11 and 12); single spirals terminating in a vine leaf (nos. 9, 10 and 13); one roundel (Fig. 41 bottom right) with a highly stylised carving in what is called a 'Cheshire cat' motif (no. 3); and one much more complex piece (Fig. 42) at the head of the arch (no. 8) which can be identified as a double vine scroll, something to be found on both Hiberno-Saxon and Romanesque sculptures.

Fig. 41: Examples of early motifs on the face of the Strata Florida abbey church western portal: left, nos. 11 and 12 on Fig. 40; top right, no. 10; bottom right, no. 3.

Fig. 42: The carving at the top of the arch (Fig. 40 no. 8). To the left is how it looks today; top right is a stylised drawing of 1889; and bottom right is an enlargement from a photograph of the 1930s.

Ornament on Key-Stone of West Doorway.

In all, these motifs on the doorway, while clearly carved by masons creating the whole ensemble, seem to be referencing something special, meaningful and ancient at a key, liminal place in the sacred geography of the building. It was designed to be distinct: once inside the church these motifs did not reappear. If so, then the project of re-creating the monastery at Strata Florida was actually preserving and re-presenting the past in a new guise, a Cistercian one: a design of structured ambiguity, another example of Rhys in partnership with the Cistercians, walking a fine line between his ancestral past and an aspirational future.

The building programme which produced the portal was working to a plan which had been laid out on the ground from the very start, consciously designing around an earlier monastery. Recent archaeological research at the abbey has now also been able to establish the overall design of the later monastery and some of its internal layout (Fig. 43).

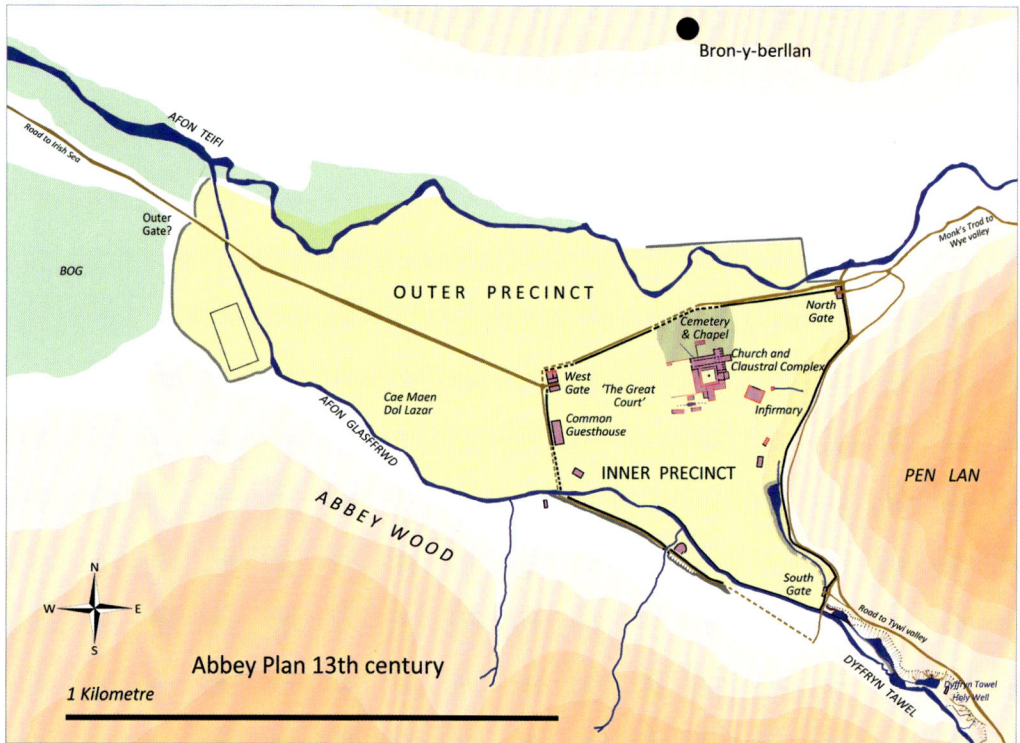

Fig. 43: The current extent of our knowledge about the layout of the abbey precinct in the mid-13th century when most of the stone buildings would have been complete.

The extent of the abbey's two precinct areas, as required by Cistercian statutes, would have been laid out and marked by an earthen bank and ditch, topped by a hedge. Later the circuit of the inner precinct area was replaced by a stone wall which still survives in places. The abbey, as it was thus laid out in the later twelfth century, was extensive, perhaps as large as 120 to 130 acres (49 to 53 ha.), making it potentially one of the largest monastic plans in Britain. As an early element of the design and construction process consideration would have been given to drainage and water management. The valley floor, while convenient for a large abbey, was nevertheless liable to flooding by the Glasffrwd and, to a lesser extent, the Teifi, especially in winter. For this reason the monks diverted the course of the Glasffrwd from its original course (see Fig. 30) into a new channel along the base of the hill to the south, all kept under control by a high retaining wall. This was connected to the upstream management system of pools and leats (see Fig. 37) and ran eastwards to a point where the river was directed northwards to meet the Teifi.

At the same time, water was provided for use in the abbey, delivered from the upstream pools by a large leat into the precinct and a header pool set on the slope about three metres above the valley floor. This drop allowed the monks to create a water mill, just beyond the header pool, which, at least later, was used as a powered forge for making iron objects. Once the power had been used the water was fed into stone-lined channels or aqueducts to convey it to various parts of the abbey complex. In recent excavations we have found the part of the aqueduct which passed along the edge of the southern range of the cloister complex of the abbey (Figs. 44 & 45).

Fig. 44: Vertical view (south to the top) of the partially-excavated aqueduct as it passed south of the main monastic ranges.

Recent excavations have also been able to extend our knowledge of the core complex of stone buildings which lay at the heart of the abbey (Fig. 45), particularly the position of the refectory and a range of buildings outside the south-west corner.

Fig. 45: Plan of the core abbey complex as understood after excavations on the south side. Walls represented in a fainter red colour are speculative reconstructions: the western range containing the lay brothers quarters is almost completely unknown.

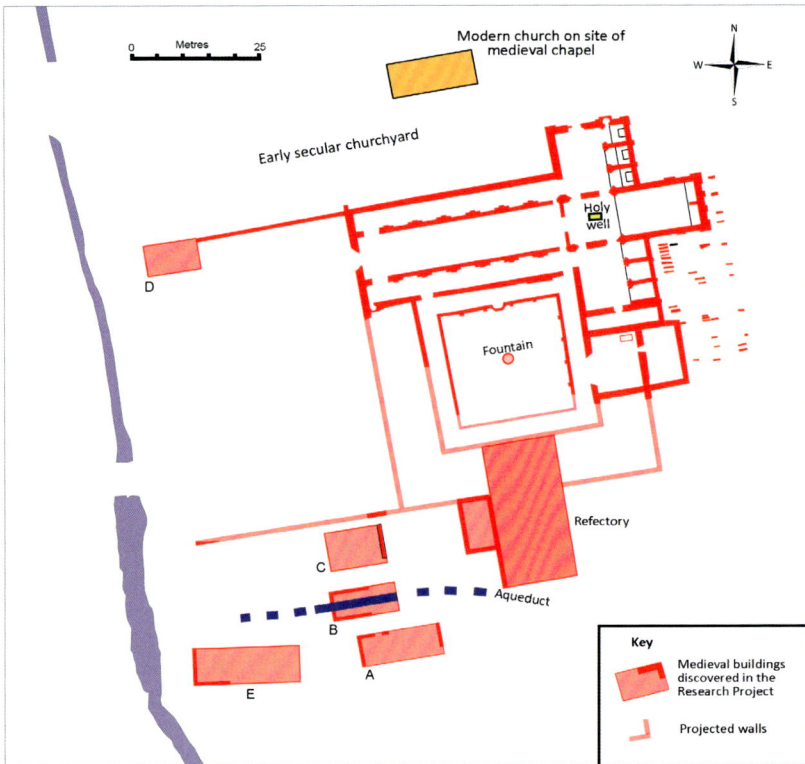

The cloister was an open courtyard garden with a fountain at its centre surrounded by an open-sided, arcarded and pentice-covered walkway ('ambulatory'), a place where, we believe, the writing desks of the scriptorium would have been placed to allow maximum light for the work of creating manuscripts of all kinds. To the east, the two-storey range contained, on the ground floor, the chapter-house and perhaps also an unlocated warming room. Above this was the dormitory for the choir monks (*monachi*), the literate and ordained priests of the order, who would access the church for the night-time offices via a stairs at the south end of the south transept. The lay brothers (*conversi*), whose major role was to provide the skilled labour for the productive tasks needed to run the abbey demesne, would have had a dormitory above the west range with store rooms on the ground floor. The lay brothers, when present, would have attended the daily offices of the abbey in the nave of the church while the choir monks officiated in the east end around the high altar and at the crossing. The south range of the cloisters had, set at right-angles to the walkway, a large refectory, with kitchens alongside, where all the monks would also come together for meals.

Beyond the core complex we know that the inner precinct contained all the other stone buildings we have so far detected. To the south-west of the core complex are four buildings which are certainly later medieval, but we have yet to discover when they were first built. We are also uncertain of the function of three of them, but one of the candidates is the Abbot's lodgings. The fourth building (E) was a large, but probably much later, barn.

Just to the north of this complex was an open courtyard in front of the west end of the abbey church with large walls to north and south. The northern wall divided the abbey complex from the grounds of the secular chapel and cemetery and at its western end was a small stone building now lying beneath the Cadw entrance museum. Elsewhere, we have discovered a substantial wall which is likely to have been part of the abbey's infirmary complex to the south-east of the church and cloisters, and to the west we have excavated the main gate between the inner and outer precincts (Fig. 46). This gatehouse was a pivotal point in the abbey plan. It was governed by the abbey's third highest official, the *portarius*, who oversaw all passage in and out of the inner precinct and its main buildings. Here the abbey's chest of coin, the treasury, was kept from which all payments were settled with merchants and traders and alms were paid to the poor and infirm. Several coins were found during the recent excavations in the room to the top right of the excavated area in Fig. 46.

Fig. 46: View, looking west, of the medieval layout of the main gatehouse between the inner and outer precincts. This was called, in a document of 1546, 'Pennyporth', probably Pen-y-porth.

To the south of the gatehouse were two other sets of buildings detected by geophysics, but as yet unexcavated. One may be a guest-house and the other a mill alongside the Afon Glasffrwd. The layout and buildings of the outer precinct of the abbey is, by contrast, largely unknown. Geophysical survey has revealed little, probably because this area would have been largely agricultural or industrial in nature with timber-framed or cob buildings which are hard to detect with this technique. It may also be an indication that this area was never completed.

Finally, there are two unusual features of the overall plan of the new abbey complex (Fig. 43). The first is the massive size of the outer precinct which may recall aspects, and perhaps even intentions, of an earlier Celtic monastic *noddfa* or sanctuary area. The other is the large open space, at least partially cobbled, between the gatehouse and the west door of the abbey church.

John Leland, the King's Antiquary, who visited the monastery just before its formal dissolution and closure in 1539, commented on this distinctive feature, saying 'the base court or camp afore the abbay is very fair and large'. This is unlike most other Cistercian abbeys, although Fountains does have a smaller version of this in the same position. It does recall the large public spaces in front of the great pilgrimage centres of Europe and there is an oral tradition that Strata Florida itself attracted pilgrims, although not officially sanctioned by the Catholic Church. Could this be related to the holy well and its celebration?

The estate and the social economy

The balancing act we have traced so far in the ways in which Strata Florida was created can also be seen in the ways in which the Cistercians managed the lands they got from their patrons. The usual pattern of organisation and administration of Cistercian estates was through granges, farms central to the manors they were granted which allowed them to farm by their own labour together with the services of their tenants to produce agricultural and other goods for their own consumption, for alms and acts of charity and for sale. In the Strata Florida landscape, however, there is no evidence for the appearance of granges, and something different seems to have happened.

The 1184 charter lists twenty names which are described as *excellentiores loci*, 'the more excellent places', which we would identify as pre-existing farms sited on the best land, stretching back into prehistory. Many of these can be instantly identified as farms which still exist and have the same names, and as such can be tracked through all the post-Dissolution rentals of the successor gentry estates up to the present day. There is, however, a small group of eight names which cannot be located in this way; they are now lost and do not appear in the post-medieval documents or on maps. However, what does appear on the maps and in the later documents is exactly the same number of other names and this all seems to be the result of a deliberate re-naming. They are a distinctive and coherent group and their new names identify specific types of agricultural production.

What seems to have happened at Strata Florida is that the abbey initially made provision for its own requirements for food, fuel and materials by taking over direct control of this group of farms, which lay in close proximity to the new abbey. They seem to have transformed these into eight specialist units as a home 'demesne' (Fig. 47). The new names, which persist until today, show how the daily needs of the monastic community were met: 1. Dôl-yr-ychain, 'the meadow of the oxen' where the main draught and meat cattle were managed; 2. Bryn-hope, 'the hill of the pigs'; 3. Dôl-beidiau, 'the meadow of the cow-sheds' (probably a dairy); 4. Dôl-fawr, 'the great meadow' (for hay); 5. Dôl-ebolion, 'the meadow of the foals' (where horses were bred); 6. Bron-y-berllan, 'the slope of the orchard' (for fruit); 7. Cae-Madog, 'Madog's field' and Cae-mawr, 'the great field' (side-by-side and taken together as one unit, the main area for producing grain). We also have archaeological evidence that the last of these 'lost' farms was actually sacrificed on the south side of the abbey precinct to create Abbey Wood to provide for all its timber needs.

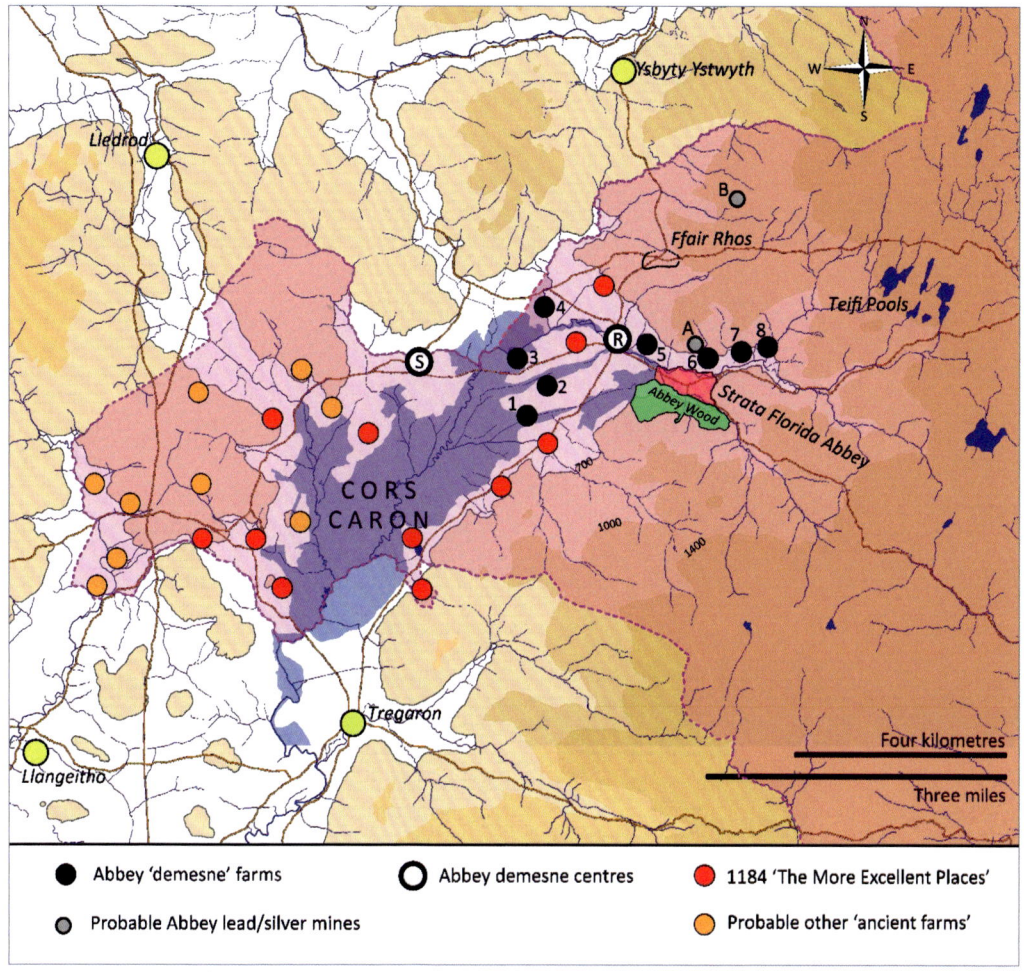

Fig. 47: The western part of the 1184 core grant to Strata Florida as it was probably reorganised by the Cistercians. On the map 'S' is Swyddffynnon and 'R' is [Pont] Rhydfendigaid.

These demesne farms probably handled some of the larger livestock: in 1295, for example, it was reckoned the monks had 428 cattle. On the great open common pastures of the Cambrian Mountains, the monks ran a flock of sheep (some 1,327 are recorded in 1295, although probably many more) operating from nearby *bercariae*, such as Troed-y-rhiw (Fig. 12), complexes with sheds, pens, and reservoirs of water for handling the animals on the *ffridd* next to the Cambrian Mountains. They took peat from Cors Caron and a number of smaller bogs nearby and on the mountain. They built ponds for fish within their complex water management systems serving the abbey precinct, but also used the natural lakes such as Teifi Pools. Within the precinct itself other plants such as legumes or nut trees would have been grown, tended by the monks themselves. This landscape of closely managed resources has left an enduring legacy in the landscape (Fig. 48).

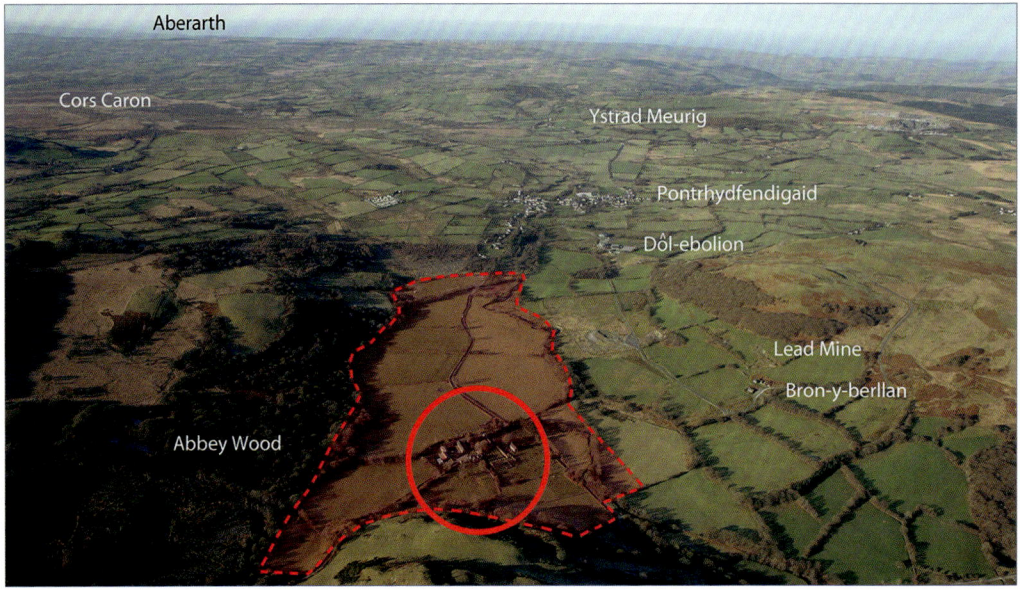

Fig. 48: Air photograph looking westwards over the abbey and its demesne lands.
The location of the abbey precinct and its main buildings are picked out in red.
In the far distance is the coastal part of the 1184 grant and Cardigan Bay.

It may be that this demesne was administered from the abbey itself with a home base within the precinct, but a stronger possibility is that the small village of Rhydfendigaid, 'the blessed ford' (now Pontrhydfendigaid) fulfilled this function. This was probably, prior to the founding of the abbey, what is called in the Welsh law codes a *maer-dref*, the administrative centre of a royal estate where a settlement of bond tenants was also placed, often close to a lord's *llys* or court (Fig. 49; 'R' on Fig. 47).

Fig. 49: A morphological analysis of [Pont] Rhydfendigaid based on the OS first edition survey of 1886. The position of the compact medieval village is picked out in red on the north side of the river. This may pre-date the 1184 re-foundation of the abbey as a maer-dref, a settlement of bond tenants run by a royal official, the maer. It is possible that the place-name Tŷ-mawr contains a reference to this officer. To this core plan was added the abbey's demesne mill served by a leat from the Teifi. To the south of the river is an area in the northwest angle of the road junction (also in red) which in 1840 was said to be 'tithe free', a designation also used of the abbey precinct. This suggests the prior existence here of an abbey holding, perhaps a hospitium for travellers on both roads.

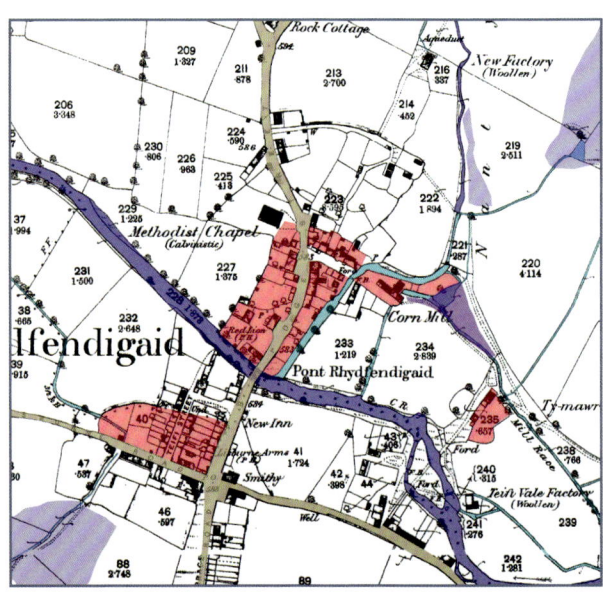

The other major element in the new landscape were the farms named in the 1184 charter that were not taken into the demesne. We also know of other farms of similar status and location which are not named in the 1184 list, but which can be found in later documents; these too can still be found in the modern landscape. For all these places (shown on Fig. 47) nothing of their medieval architectures survives and the archaeology of what was once there is, probably, hidden beneath the yards and buildings (eighteenth-century and later) of the modern farms. On rare occasions, however, such as the drought of 2018, we can see crop-marks of the earlier farms and their enclosures appearing out from underneath the modern successors as at Llwyn-y-gog (Fig. 50).

Fig. 50: Air photograph of crop-marks at Llwyn-y-gog taken during the drought of July 2018. Llwyn-y-gog is one of the ancient farms named in the charter of 1184 as excellentiores loci ('the more excellent places'). On Fig. 47 it is the northernmost red circle.

Although the abbey has little surviving medieval documentation, we can, perhaps, assume that these places continued to be farmed by the Welsh men and women who had done so in previous generations by hereditary right. Their tenurial relationship with the abbey was likely to have been the same as it had been with their princes. It would also seem that the abbey had at least one central place for administering these other farms, another *maer-dref*, granted as 'Ffynnon Oer', but later re-named Swyddffynnon (Fig. 51), probably associated previously with the royal *llys* at Ystrad Meurig. Here there was a chapel, probably one of the pre-Norman *llan* sites of the *clas* system (Fig. 47 'S') and a mill. It was also conveniently located on the Lôn Lacs routeway between Strata Florida and Aberarth, as was Rhydfendigaid.

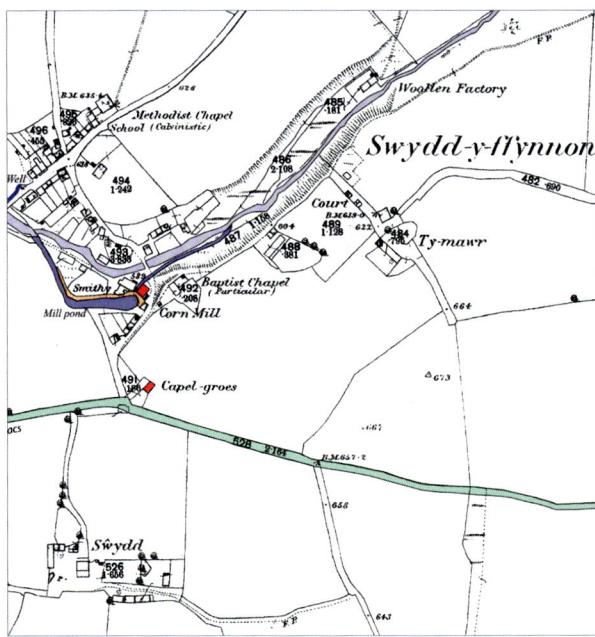

Fig. 51: Swyddffynnon: 25-inch-to-the-mile OS map showing also: the medieval mill pond, its dam (orange symbol) and tail race; mill building (red); early chapel site; Lôn Lacs; and holy well. Together with place-names, Tŷ-mawr, Court, Capel-groes and Swydd, these sketch out the probable topography of the medieval administrative centre using an earlier maer-dref.

Thus, in the first phase of the abbey, from the twelfth to the end of the thirteenth centuries, we can see that the monks were careful not to change too much in the social economy, except for its core demesne and their large flocks of sheep sharing the common upland pastures with their tenants using their own rights of access. At first, therefore, out in the wider countryside, much must have seemed to the people of Strata Florida's region to be carried out as it had been in the preceding century or more. The abbey took its dues from free and bond families alike, but these obligations were essentially those that had been transferred to the abbey from secular princes and noblemen through the charters and land grants. The abbey took the product of these obligations mostly as agricultural goods, known as *gwestfa*. It also took services of all kinds: from the bond tenants, as labour working with the lay brothers on the demesne farms or on building and maintenance, and free tenants who would carry goods and act as servants or secular officials within the precincts and on the estate. Thus in the locality the familiar structures of social interaction would have continued. From this interaction the abbey also took revenue, such as through engagement with legal action with its exactions of fines and penalties. There were also other long-established sources of income, known as 'spiritualities', including tithes and gifts of piety. The Cistercians of Strata Florida, in these ways, run largely by monks of Welsh background, felt their way into managing this landscape, respecting, for a while at least, time-honoured custom and practice.

We can illustrate some of the details of this by comparing two maps which attempt to summarise the landscape layout of the abbey's environs as it might have appeared before (Fig. 52) and after (Fig. 53) the re-foundation in 1184. This is the area of the abbey landscape most altered by the arrival of the Cistercians.

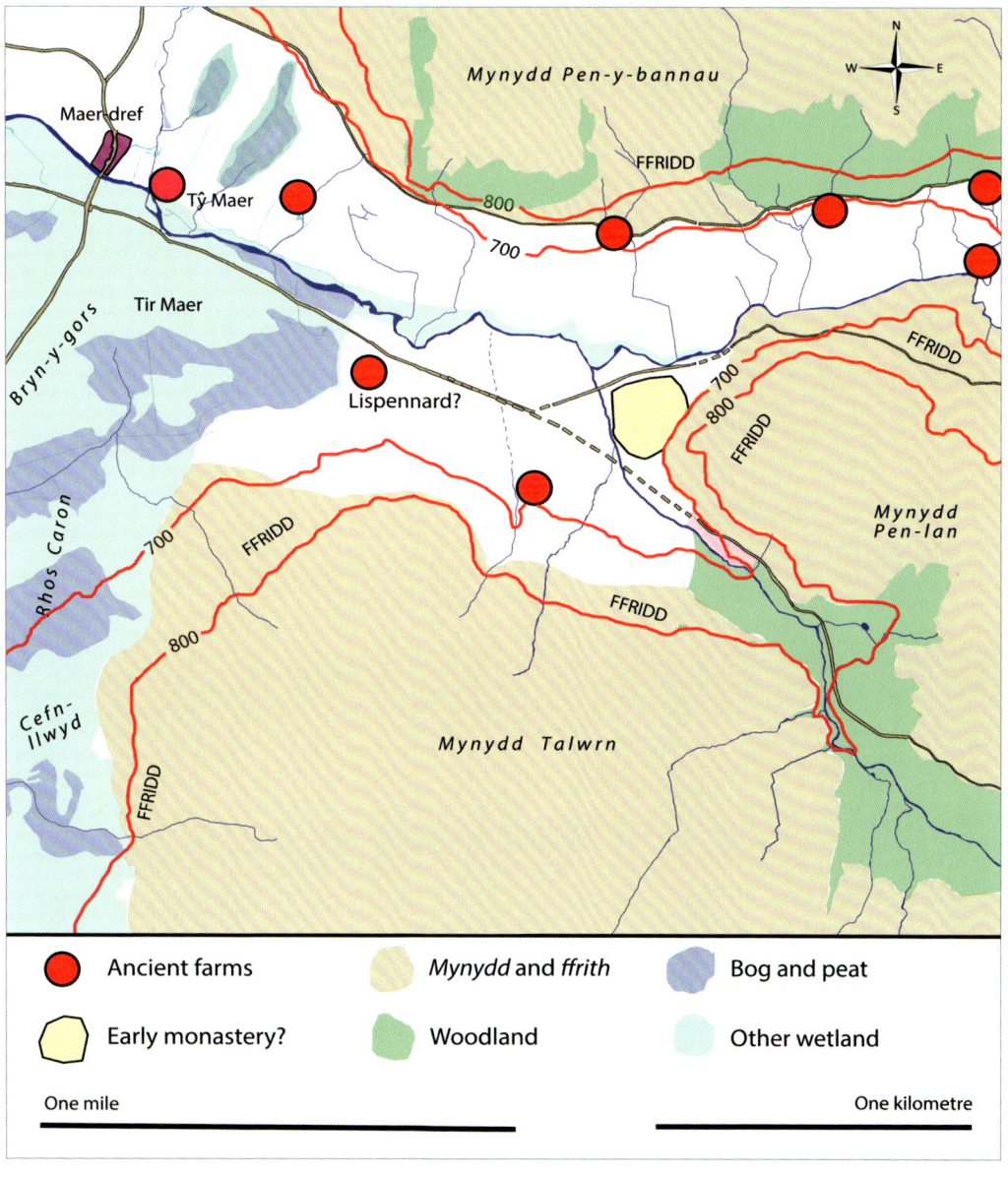

Fig. 52: A tentative mapping of the abbey's immediate landscape at the end of the eleventh and beginning of the twelfth centuries. This is based on the premise that the farms (red circles) are among those named in the 1184 charter as 'excellentiores loci'. This includes an hypothesized location for Lispennard, named in 1164, but gone in 1184 presumably because it was subsumed within the abbey precinct. It shows also the nearby bond maerdref of [Pont]Rhydfendigaid. The 700-foot contour is used as the approximate position, in this locality and at this date, of the boundary between the cultivated farmlands (white on the map) and the mynydd and ffridd of the upland pastures. The road lines are reconstructed on archaeological and morphological evidence and the position of the projected earlier monastery is picked out in yellow.

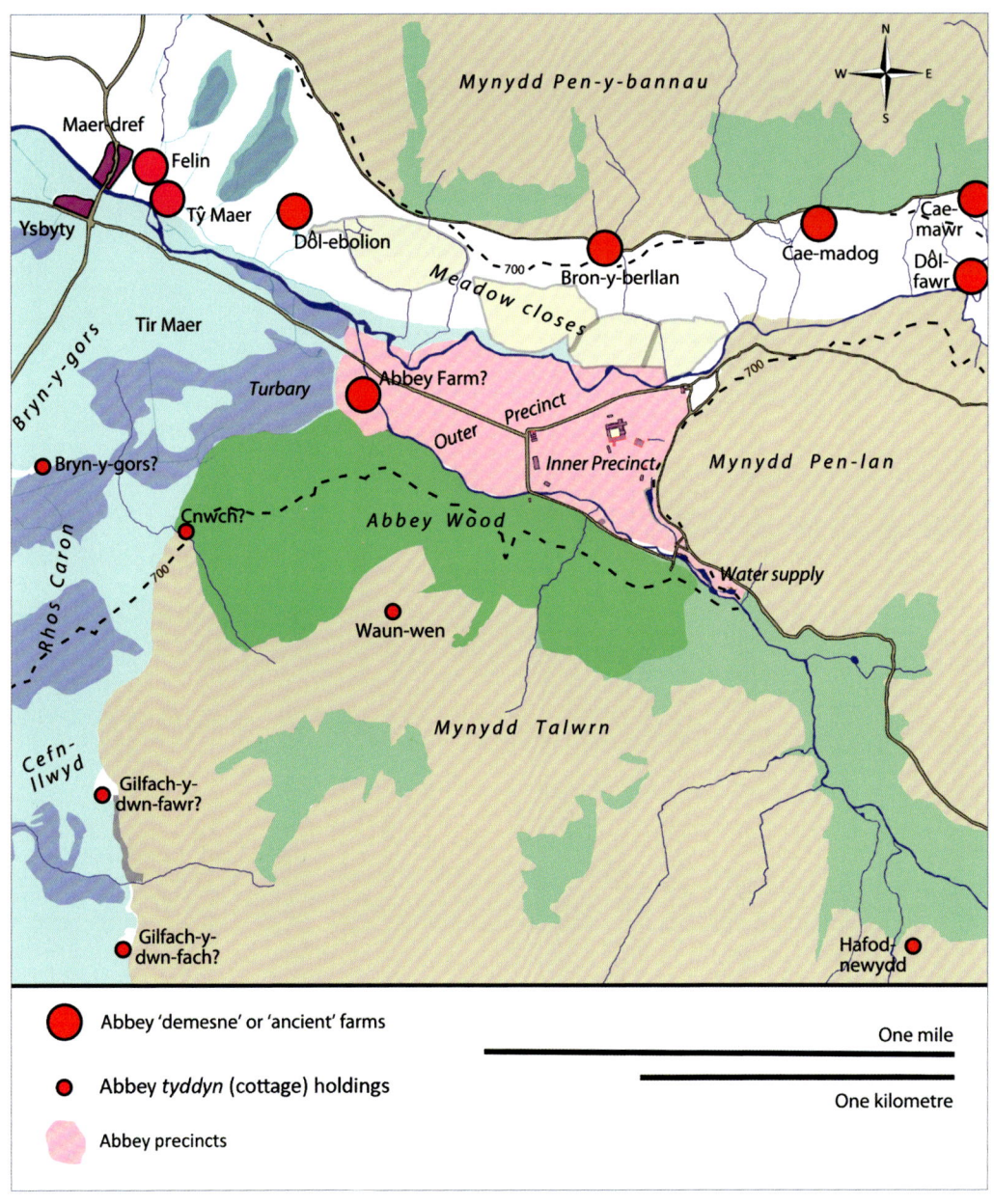

Fig. 53: A slightly less tentative mapping of the abbey landscape by the thirteenth century. The ancient farms had become part of the abbey's specialist demesne and the maer-dref its village for bond tenants. The precinct at its fullest extent is shown with the rearranged road system, 'by-passing' the inner precinct with the principal buildings and the newly planned Abbey Wood which archaeology has shown was planted over an earlier farm and its field systems. The 'meadow closes' are likely to have originated as paddocks associated with Dôl-ebolion, the abbey's horse-breeding farm.

It was all very well, however, managing local resources for internal needs and systems, but Strata Florida was part of a European institution in its scope and experience. It had to engage with the wider world and for this it needed cash. Right from the start it bought its best building stone from commercial quarries in Dundry, Somerset as well as other materials unavailable locally; these all had their price. The abbey's Cellarer, its chief managerial officer, working with its Porter, the keeper of the treasury at the gate, would have had the constant need to find money. It was their responsibility to sustain not only the monastic community, but also the sick and dying, the poor at the gate and the pensioners (*corrodians*). It was their responsibility also to provide wine for the altar and the abbot's table, or metal and ceramic vessels and cloth for the richer vestments. There were other institutional demands: as early as 1212, for example, the abbey had to find the huge sum of £800 imposed by King John which it took forty years to pay off.

An important consideration here is that, as the abbey began its life, this part of Wales was on the periphery of state-controlled money and market economies. The currency in circulation was English, but it was probably little used in everyday life in the twelfth century. There was no regulation of trade and coinage as there had been in the English laws since the seventh century, and there were no identifiable organised market centres in the Teifi valley. This was because Deheubarth was not a centralized state in the English or Marcher manner and as such did not generate documents for the conduct of everyday life. This must have seemed strange to senior Cistercian officials who were, elsewhere, creating monasteries mostly within European feudal states with bureaucratic establishments capable of governing over large areas by the use of written commands and constant exaction of money. In the pre-existing Welsh landscape there was an official spatial organisation into commotes and cantrefs for the purposes of administering the law and enabling the flow of renders, but these seem to have been managed by noble elites (*uchelwyr*) and local power brokers acting as ministers to their prince. This deficiency in the organization of the body politic of Wales to some extent restricted the abbey's capacity to generate coin for its own treasury, and so where would it have come from?

One key contributor would have been trade. In this context it is noticeable that Strata Florida established its own market place, at Ffair Rhos on the hill above the abbey, but not as a European style borough with resident traders and manufacturers in a planned and permanent settlement. It seems to have been a large enclosure on the open moorland (*rhos*) set astride an ancient junction of routeways (Fig. 54).

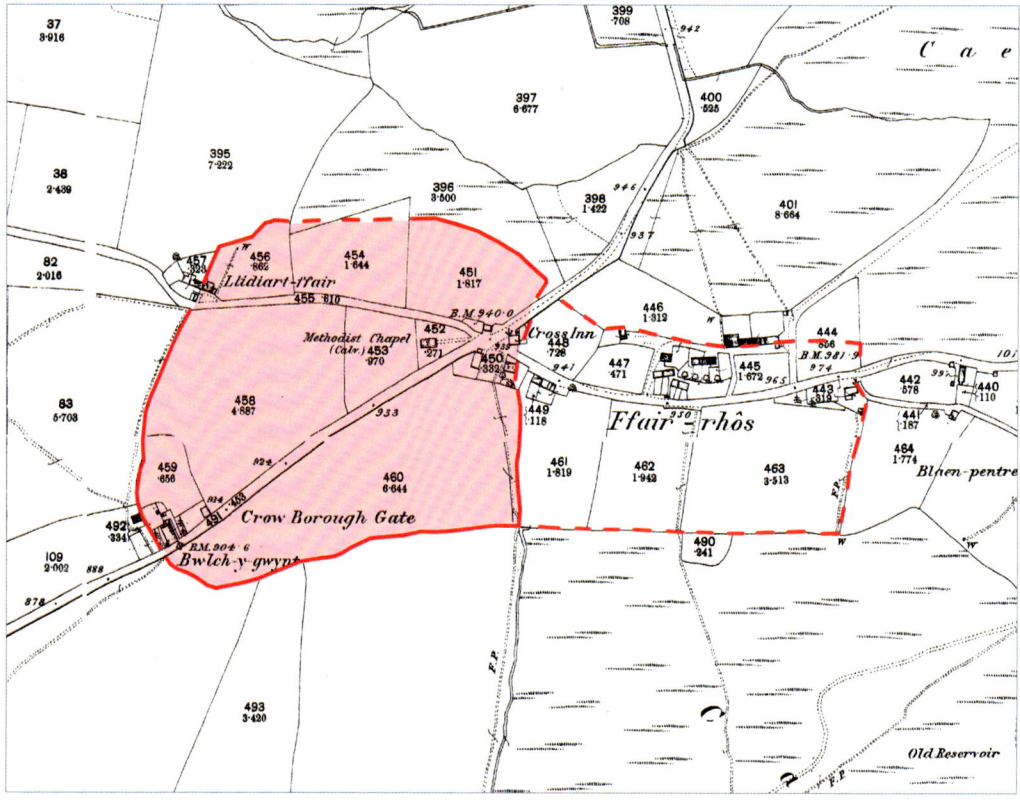

Fig. 54: Ffair Rhos ('Fair on the moor') on first edition 25-inch to the mile OS survey of 1886. The shaded enclosure exists, for the most part, as a clear curvilinear embankment and has the place-names of two gates which once allowed access to it (Llidiart-ffair and Crow Borough Gate). The eastern edge, however, is uncertain, as was its relationship with the small settlement of Ffair Rhos itself which seems to have had its own defining boundaries. It may be that the whole of the area was all part of the original fair legalized after 1284 as a borough under English law.

Trading here was probably in livestock and perhaps seasonal as animals were moved along well-established transhumant routes and then traded. They were places to hold occasional and seasonal operations, 'fairings', where itinerant traders would also turn up to sell or exchange certain manufactured goods as they may well have done for centuries (Fig. 55).

Fig. 55: An 'occasional' sheep sale at Devil's Bridge 2000.

Fig. 55: An 'occasional' sheep sale at Devil's Bridge 2000.

The Cistercians would thus have been regularising something indigenous to the Welsh upland culture. It would take well into the next century, however, for the establishment of organised fixed settlements and for specialist manufacture and trading of goods to come into this part of the world. Locally-made pottery, for example, makes no appearance on our archaeological site until the later thirteenth or fourteenth centuries.

This sense that the monks of Strata Florida had to construct a world that would fit their cash needs can be found when we look again at both the 1164 and the 1184 grant. Built into the structure of the documents were not only grants of land with significant agrarian capacity, but also a point of access to the sea and its resources. In 1184, it is specifically stated that the Lord Rhys granted fish weirs or traps along the shoreline between Aberarth and Aberaeron (Fig. 56).

Fig. 56: Shoreline to the south of Aberarth with fish-trapping area shaded in yellow. The stone structure of the fish-weirs can be seen just outside the shaded area.

The sea, more importantly, here the Irish Sea, was the super highway of its day allowing the movement of people and goods over long distances, especially with mountain roads and passes difficult, dangerous and ill-serviced. In particular, their introduction of large flocks of sheep was predicated on getting their wool to international markets, many at the time in the great weaving centres of mainland Europe, such as Flanders. The nearest conventional port at the time would have been Cardigan, but elsewhere along the rocky coastline of Cardigan Bay it was very difficult to construct harbours. Thus although the land granted to Strata Florida on the coast at Aberarth was the shortest distance to the sea at the western end of an ancient routeway passing through the new abbey site, called the Lôn Lacs, there was no harbour. Any trading vessel would have had to beach on the stony shore at slack water at the end of high tide, load and unload at low and then re-float with the returning tide, something still seen up to the end of the nineteenth century (Fig. 57).

Fig. 57: Coastal trading smacks beached at Traeth-y-llongau, Aberporth c.1890.

Trade alone could not, however, have generated the levels of cash that the abbey was handling almost from the start. There would have been gifts of money or loans from patrons and wealthy travellers, including pilgrims, enjoying the abbey's reputation for hospitality, but none of this is recorded for Strata Florida. Nonetheless there would also have been the need for innovation to embed its cash generating within the fabric of its estate. We can suspect, therefore, that from early on the abbey gradually began the switch from income in kind to income in cash. How and when renders became rents and court fines and church dues began to be paid in coin we simply do not know, but this may have happened earlier than we think, perhaps even from the beginning. One such may be the *commorth*, the render made every three years by the abbey's tenants for access to the common pastures.

These permanent and extensive rough pasture lands were an essential part of the farming rhythm of the year. Stock was sent onto upland pastures between May-day and Michaelmas to keep them away from the crops growing on the lowland fields. Here they were tended, milked and dairy products made in the *hafodydd*, 'summer houses' and *lluestau* 'huts' before the animals were taken down to the farms to over-winter and manure the intensively cultivated fields and meadows. The *hafodydd* were to be found originally on the *ffridd*, lying between the open moorland and the lowland fields, where they would also have had small areas of crops such as legumes. These later formed the basis for the steady expansion of more permanent settlement into the upland.

The introduction of improved technology may also have eased the path of fiscal change. For example, the archaeology seems to support the view that it was the Cistercians in this part of the world who introduced more advanced hydrological management to drain marshland, divert rivers, manage water supply and power mills. This we have seen most clearly in and around the precinct of the abbey, but the monks also constructed major mills at key locations, such as Rhydfendigaid (Fig. 49) and Swyddffynnon (Fig. 51), where tenants would have been compelled to grind their corn and be levied for the privilege, all to boost the monks' income, but linked also to the existing working practices of local people.

The abbey after Lord Rhys

We can see that the Cistercians, in addition to bringing reformed monasticism, helped also in the process of bringing the outside world of market economies, new husbandry practices, bureaucracy and European institutional management to central Wales. Yet it was also intended that the traditional world should continue at least partly as a Welsh monastery operating in a Welsh way among its communities and regional power-brokers. Rhys's balancing act did not last for long, however, and the old ways very quickly led to his downfall. To preserve any notion he might have had of building a stable Welsh state in Deheubarth with Strata Florida as its administrative heart, he would have needed to ensure its transfer to the next generation intact as a unified territory under one administration. For this, primogeniture, the inheritance of all powers and jurisdictions by his eldest son alone, as in European feudal law, would have been essential. Under Welsh law and social practice, however, all his sons would have felt that they were due at least a part of the inheritance. This tension broke surface even in Rhys's lifetime. When Henry II died in 1189, Rhys no longer felt bound by the agreement of 1171 and attacked the Anglo-Norman lordships of the March, but even before his own death in 1197 he had to deal also with the ambitions of his sons. His designated legitimate heir, Gruffudd, was opposed by the eldest, but illegitimate son, Maelgwn, who, under Welsh law, had as much right to some part of the inheritance as all his other eight brothers. Gruffudd tried to consolidate his hold over the whole of Deheubarth by having his succession confirmed by the Justiciar of England, but this failed and a long period of warfare began which drew in neighbouring princes and marcher lords. In 1216 the increasingly dominant Llywelyn ap Iorwerth of Gwynedd who exercised a strong degree of control in Ceredigion allocated portions of Deheubarth to Rhys's sons and grandsons. This did not end the matter, however, and the descendants of Rhys were still contesting and dividing his dwindling realm late into the thirteenth century.

In these turbulent circumstances the community at Strata Florida must have felt a deal of insecurity, fearing that their estate would be eroded by conflict and ambition. Their defence was to request, and probably prepare, documents confirming, and effectively re-issuing, previous charters. Fortunately for us this continued into the later Middle Ages with confirmations sought from, and given by, successive English kings. In this way the early charters of the princes of Deheubarth were recorded, thus preserving information which would otherwise have been lost.

Despite all this, Rhys's successors actually continued to strengthen Strata Florida well into the thirteenth century by giving additional land. This completed an impressive footprint of landscape control at the centre of Wales, consisting of extensive land holdings, rights of access to large swathes of upland pastures and income from two major appropriated churches at Llangurig and Pencarreg (Fig. 58).

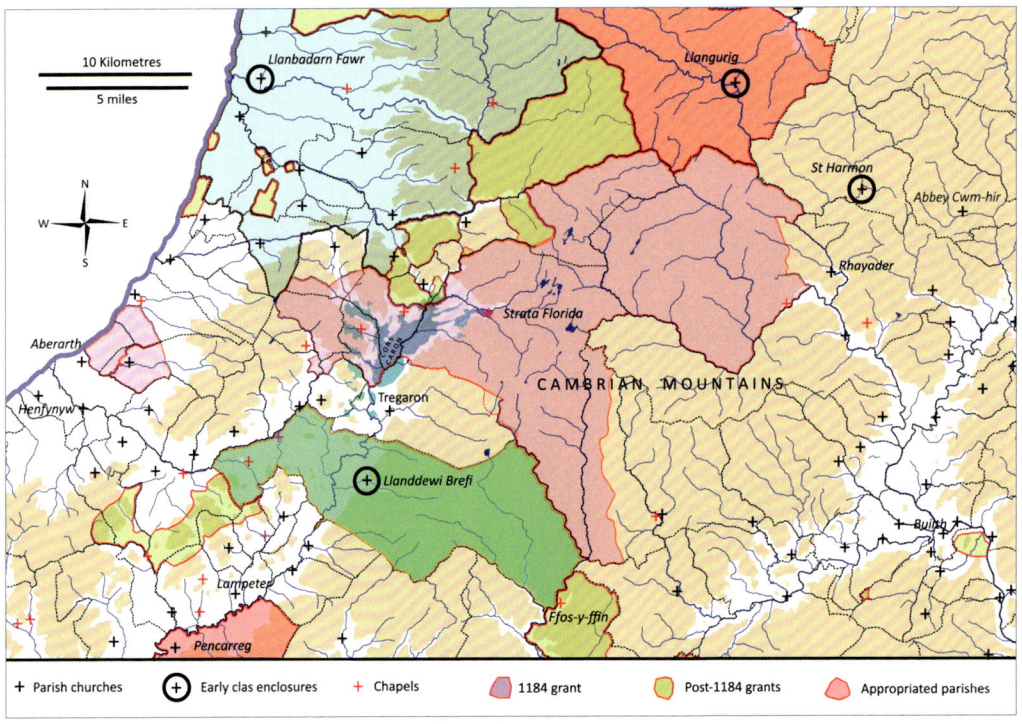

Fig. 58: Lands controlled by Strata Florida in mid-Wales by the mid-thirteenth century. This does not indicate the grant (1202 by Rhys Ieuanc ap Gruffudd) of additional rights of access to pasture on the uplands of Cantref Penweddig (broadly the lands of Llanbadarn) and the other three cantrefs of Ceredigion, as well as Cantref Bychan and Cantref Mawr in north Carmarthenshire.

Occasionally the land does come into view in the surviving documents, but usually as records of disputes resolved in English courts. In the thirteenth century, for example, there were land disputes with other Cistercian abbeys as they also settled into their new lands. They sometimes came into close contact with each other, and boundaries were contested, often in the unfenced uplands, as with Cwm-hir, Neath and Dore. However, there were also disputes arising from the regional warfare following the death of

Rhys when secular descendants tried to reverse grants and retrieve holdings which had permanently transferred to Strata Florida. There was just such a case with nearby Ystrad Meurig and the commote of Mefenydd, when one of Rhys's grandsons, Maelgwn ap Maelgwn, tried to retrieve it and partially succeeded.

The abbey was well able to deal with these occasional disturbances because of Latin monasticism's long experience of administration and meticulous record keeping, and the late twelfth and thirteenth centuries saw its hey-day. Gerald of Wales, writing in 1216 was already able to say that Strata Florida 'was in the course of time enriched far more abundantly with oxen, studs of horses, herds of cattle and flocks of sheep, and the riches they produced, than all the houses of the same order throughout Wales'. In 1191 he had already said of the Cistercians; 'settle them in some barren retreat which is hidden away in a wilderness or forest and a year or two later you will find a splendid church there and fine monastic buildings, with a great deal of property and all the wealth you can imagine'.

Fig. 59: The great slab found in the chapter-house in the Williams excavations of the 1880s.

Indeed by the time that the monks entered their new church in 1201, it was complete, although the east end was re-modelled very soon after, and over the next generation the buildings around the cloister followed. How much else had been completed is uncertain apart for the great gate which was also up and functioning at an early stage. Another early element, as we have seen, were the burials to be found in the angle between the south transept and the presbytery at the east end of the church. In all, the *Brut y Tywysogion* (Chronicle of the Princes) before 1222 recorded five burials of members of Lord Rhys's family as well as another two of the region's secular elite and one abbot, all probably in external graves. After that, up to 1275, another ten of the Deheubarth dynasty were buried there, but in the chapter-house. Two of these burials were of women, Matilda de Breos, a woman of aristocratic Anglo-Norman lineage married to Gruffudd ap Rhys, and Gwenllian, daughter of Maelgwn 'Ieuanc' ap Maelgwn. In the nineteenth-century excavation of the chapter-house a large pit with multiple burials in it, including at least twelve skulls, was found covered by an ornate cross-carved slab: this might have been an interment of all the noble remains when this building was being re-modelled (Fig. 59).

Its role as a mausoleum for the royal line must have been a clear intention from the start and matches the status of the abbey as we find it in documents throughout the Middle Ages. This reputational high standing began so early that it may have acquired some of its prestige from its possible clas predecessor. Two events are of particular note in telling how the abbey was regarded. In 1212, King John ordered his castellans of Cardigan, Carmarthen and Gower to destroy Strata Florida 'so far as you are able' because it 'sustains our enemies'. He clearly saw something potentially dangerous to English interests and helpful to Welsh emerging in the far west. Then in 1238, two years before his death, Llywelyn 'Fawr' ap Iorwerth, Prince of Gwynedd, used Strata Florida for a very special occasion, summoning all the princes of Wales to the abbey to swear 'allegiance and fealty' to his son and chosen heir, Dafydd, a feudal act. As with Rhys a generation earlier, the intention was to enable primogeniture (succession of the first-born son) and ensure the intact transfer of a state. It is of great significance that Llywelyn chose to do this not in Gwynedd, but at a location in the heart of Pura Wallia already associated perhaps with the aspiration to be the centre of a Welsh state.

Not surprisingly, therefore, we find the abbots of Strata Florida, along with their peers in other Cistercian houses, taking some leadership in the politics of Wales. In 1200 and 1216, for example, they were corresponding with the Pope; in 1201 they had urged Madog ap Gruffudd Maelor to found Valle Crucis abbey; in 1248 the abbot of Strata Florida worked with the abbot of Aberconwy, its daughter house, to retrieve the body of Gruffudd ap Llywelyn from the Tower of London; and in 1270 nearly all the abbots of the Whitland family of Cistercians wrote to Pope Gregory X defending the position taken by Llywelyn ap Gruffudd of Gwynedd against Edward I.

Perhaps, however, the greatest and the most enduring of all Strata Florida's claims to fame was its support of the idea of Wales through its language and literary culture. Between 1250 and 1350, there was a massive expansion, from none to about sixty, in the number of surviving manuscripts containing texts in the Welsh language. By about 1400, according to Daniel Huws, 'almost everything we treasure of early Welsh literature had been recorded'. At the heart of this revolution we can place the Whitland family of Cistercians with Strata Florida perhaps the most prominent among them. It is hard, with total certainty, to ascribe any one manuscript to any particular scriptorium but scholars think that the original Latin version of the *Brut y Tywysogion* was begun at Llanbadarn Fawr and then continued and translated into Welsh at Strata Florida (Fig. 60). It is the first history of Wales in the vernacular language of the country.

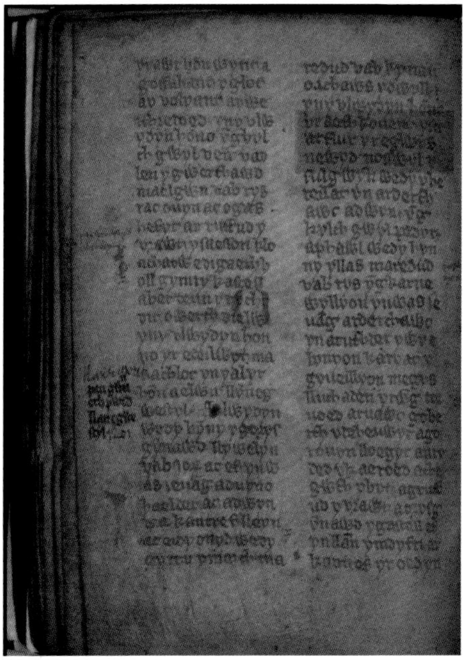

Fig. 60: The *Brut* entry for 1201 with the reference to the monks entering their new church highlighted.

Fig. 61: A page from the Hendregadredd Manuscript, with part of a twelfth-century poem by Owain Cyfeiliog of Powys in the hand of the original Strata Florida scribe c. 1300, and the beginning of a poem by Dafydd ap Gwilym (c. 1315 – c. 1350), most probably in his own hand, added later in a blank space underneath.

Such an act of compilation is almost certainly true also of one of the most important collections of early Welsh poetry, the Hendregadredd Manuscript (Fig. 61), consciously crafted initially in the scriptorium of Strata Florida as a demonstration of the 'Poets of the Princes', including representative examples of the best up to the death of Llywelyn 'the Last' in 1282. The manuscript seems then to have passed into the hands of Ieuan Llwyd of Glyn Aeron, whose great-grandfather was buried at Strata Florida. One other manuscript can also be associated with the abbey: the White Book of Rhydderch, commissioned by (or for) Rhydderch the son of Ieuan Llwyd, hence the manuscript's name. It is the oldest document containing more or less complete copies of the *Mabinogi* and other prose tales.

Other manuscripts including parts of the Red Book of Hergest may be traced back to original texts held at Strata Florida. All of this, it might be suggested, seems to have been part of a conscious strategy not only of preserving the best of early Welsh literature, but also of establishing a body of work which could act as a foundation layer of Welsh culture within a Welsh nation. This is all of a piece with knowing that the Cistercian abbots were themselves patrons of poets and their work, the earliest recorded being Abbot Llywelyn of Strata Florida in the mid-fourteenth century.

All of this cultural activity seems to have continued throughout what even contemporaries saw was a crisis for the 'Welsh project'. As a result of two concerted campaigns in 1276-7 and 1282-3 led by Edward I of England the lands of the princes of Gwynedd and Deheubarth were brought into the crown demesne, and the Statute of Rhuddlan in 1284 began the process of making Wales subject more closely to the Kings of England. For Strata Florida instability increased, albeit protected still by its role as a Cistercian institution within the body politic of Latin Christendom. In 1278 Strata Florida was forced to give up land for the building of Aberystwyth Castle; the abbot had to seek redress from the king for trying to erode its customary privilege and its estate; and in 1283 the abbot even had to seek letters of protection for his people 'buying victuals for the maintenance of their house'. The Crown also, in 1278, 1280 and 1284, required the abbey to cut back its woodlands, especially along the lines of roads, since they were places used for attack by Welsh forces (Fig. 62).

Fig. 62: The Monk's Trod passing through modern woodland. These were the stretches of the routeways crossing the Welsh uplands and coming down through steep-sided wooded valleys which English edicts wanted felled at the end of the thirteenth century.

On the other hand the authority of the abbots in negotiating the changes was also important, bridging as they did between their local prestige and their international standing. Thus in 1281, Abbot Philip of Strata Florida was recruited with others to be involved in a crown enquiry about Welsh law, perhaps as preparation for the involvement of English administrators more closely in the affairs of the Welsh landscape. Maybe too this role continued as the abbot of Strata Florida was summoned, between 1295 and 1307, to the English parliament on seven occasions, far more than any other Welsh Cistercian.

With the Statute of Rhuddlan in 1284 the patronage of Strata Florida passed unrecorded into English royal hands, a role recognized in the inspections and confirmations of the original charters of the abbey. Such validation from the new power was essential to the abbey. This fundamental change in the order of things was curiously symbolized by what seems to have been an act of God; in 1284, English and Welsh chroniclers describe in great detail the burning of Strata Florida church after the crossing tower had been struck by lightning. Accounts suggest that it was most destructive at the east end where the timber roofing of the belfry tower (at the crossing) and the transepts was destroyed as well as 'the choir books' kept in the narrow room between the south transept and the chapter-house (Fig. 63). Nineteenth century excavations revealed that molten lead from the burning roof had oozed down through the walls of the church (Fig. 64).

Fig. 63: The narrow room between the south transept of the church and the chapter-house (to the right) which probably housed the choir books destroyed in the 1284 fire.

Fig. 64: Molten lead from the church walls found in the nineteenth-century excavations.

This was not, however, the end of destruction. During the uprising by Madog ap Llewelyn of Gwynedd in 1295, Abbot Anian Sais of Strata Florida had promised that he would bring the Ceredigion contingent of the rebellion to submit to the king, itself an indication of local secular leadership. He failed, however, and in retaliation Edward I ordered his forces to burn the countryside, with one chronicler saying how both abbey and country were in flames. It may well be that it was not the church which suffered again, but some of the more peripheral buildings. Recent excavations have shown, for example, that the main gate at least was intensely burned at this time. However, this second destructive episode was represented by the king as being against his will, when he sanctioned, in 1300, the monks 'to rebuild on its former site their abbey which was burned in the Welsh war'. However, the fact that Strata Florida was attacked in this way may suggest a deliberate act of war perhaps against an institution which continued, as King John had put it in 1212, to harbour the enemies of the crown.

Making adjustments: the later abbey

Perhaps as a conscious and strategic act in reaction to these events and perhaps because recruitment of monks was falling, the decision was taken to reduce the physical presence of the abbey and its precinct in the landscape, pulling back from the aspirations set out at the foundation. This adjustment meant an adaptation to the new circumstances in the political and social milieu after 1284. Thus, the work of rebuilding the church seems, in reality, to have been limited to relatively superficial restoration. This involved new tiles being bought from kilns in the upper Severn valley to be put on the floors of the transept chapels, crossing and presbytery (Fig. 65), as well as the re-vaulting of the transepts and fresh lime-wash for the walls.

Fig. 65: An early fourteenth-century encaustic tile, depicting a man in woodland holding a mirror or, alternatively, a 'cadge', a ring for trained hawks to perch on during hunting.

It may well be that it was at this point too that the Outer Precinct was abandoned, even before anything much had been built there. It probably became an area of specialist agricultural activity, although we have to notice that a place-name recorded in 1765, Cae Maen y Dol Lazar, may refer to a leper hospital in this area. The excavation of the great gate has also shown that this was expanded and given a new floor, to become the main entrance to a less ambitious abbey plan (Fig. 66).

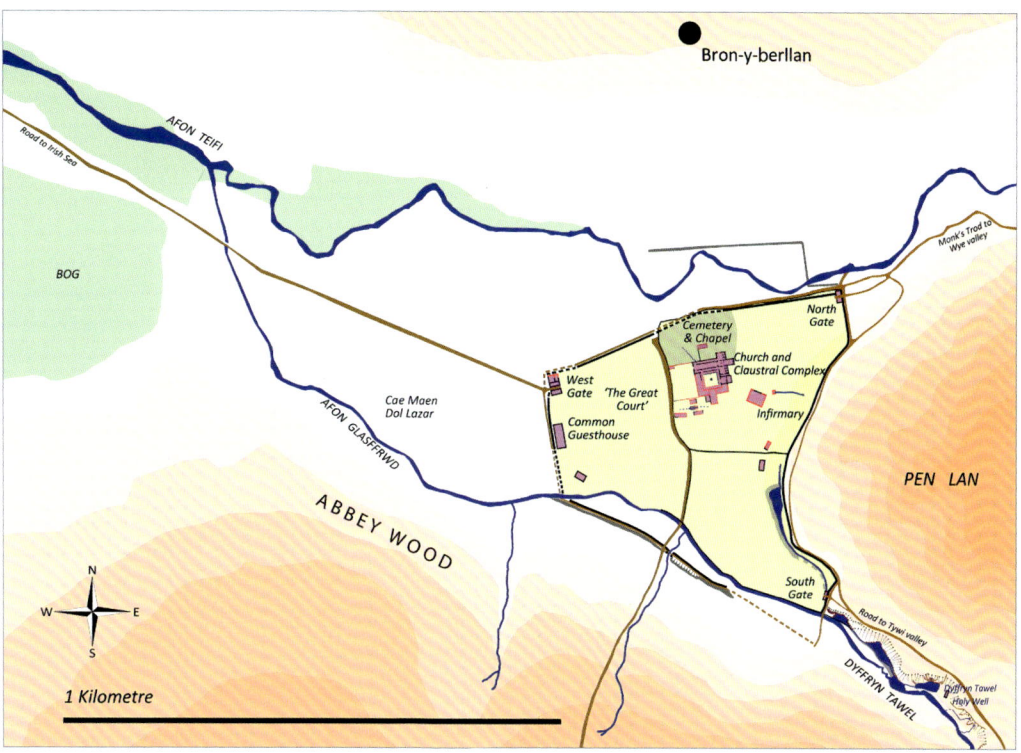

Fig. 66: Plan of the abbey in the fourteenth century.

There is no doubt that the end of the thirteenth century saw material catastrophe and fresh jeopardy in the world in which Strata Florida existed and operated, but we must be careful not to see this as a simple record of decline which ended with the Dissolution in 1539. The documentary sources, by their very nature, tend to highlight the bad things that happen. By contrast the poets of the fourteenth and fifteenth centuries who saw and spent time within its walls made no mention of decline, rather they celebrated the place as a wonder and a vibrant and active monastery continuing to play its part in the world. We should, therefore, see the later Middle Ages as a time of adaptation and resilience, constantly re-defining its role in changing circumstances.

We have already been able to track this process of adaptation for its early years and five inter-related themes have emerged: the nature and meaning of the abbey's physical presence in the world; its prestige and status within the various body politics from local to international; its actions in the structures of the agrarian economy and social ordering; its role in the cultural production of Wales; and its complex identity as a spiritual centre, giving human access to what lies beyond.

There were, it must be admitted, fierce pressures on the abbey in the later Middle Ages, one of which was the requirement by the English state to provide more money for the public purse. So, between 1336 and 1344, for example, Edward, the 'Black Prince' of Wales, tried to levy money by arguing that the abbey should be paying for its unfulfilled feudal obligation to serve on the royal courts in Cardigan, from which actually it was exempt. This worsened in the fifteenth century when the state and the papacy used, with increasing frequency, the device of levying *ad hoc* 'subsidies' to cover their escalating costs, often using heads of monastic houses as 'collectors' of these unpopular taxes. If they failed to get the money out of a reluctant populace, the abbots were obliged to find the shortfall. This happened four times in the 1430s and in the end Abbot Rhys was imprisoned in Carmarthen for failure to pay his debt, dying there in 1440-1, but not before wealth had already drained from the abbey's chests.

Then there was starvation and pandemic. In the early fourteenth century there were famines throughout Britain brought about by crop failure and severe cattle murrains devastating livestock. This was followed, in 1349 and for another twenty years, by the Black Death, hitting an already weakened and depleted population. We have little information for mid-Wales, but we do know that between 30% and 40% of the population of the British Isles died and we have no reason to believe that it was any different in the abbey closes and among the farms of Strata Florida.

Next, as ever, there was warfare with one notable occurrence: the war the English crown had with Owain Glyndŵr which began in 1400. The monks of Strata Florida may well have decided to support this claimant of the title 'Prince of Wales' and they paid the price. On three separate occasions, elements of the English armies pursuing Glyndŵr were billeted within the monastery at Strata Florida. In 1401 Henry IV's army stayed for a month and the *Chronicle of Adam of Usk* reported that 'the church and choir right up to the high altar was converted into a stable and completely stripped of its plate'. As a result the abbey became 'greatly impoverished and the lands devastated by English and Welsh alike'. So bad was it that Henry IV in 1402, as an act of protection, took custody of the abbey and all its assets, putting it into the administration of the Earl of Worcester until 1415. Then in 1407 120 men-at-arms and 360 archers stayed for three months, while in 1415 a contingent of 40 men-at-arms and 80 archers were housed at Strata Florida. The monks eventually claimed in 1442 that 'their house was so spoiled by Owain and the Welsh rebels, the walls of the church excepted, that the same could not be repaired without the king's aid'.

But there were good times too which often went almost completely unrecorded. Certain abbots had long tenures, notably Llywelyn Fychan (1340s to c. 1382), Rhys ap Dafydd ap Llewelyn (c. 1416-1441) and Morgan ap Rhys (1444-1486) and were picked out for praise in their own times. Llywelyn Fychan, after a turbulent start, went on to govern a seemingly peaceful era and when, in 1377, Richard II confirmed the appropriation of Pencarreg parish, he said that it had been done 'in consideration of the high place the abbot held with [the Black Prince] and now holds with us'. Rhys ap Dafydd was from a noble lineage who were lords of Caeo only 21 miles to the south of Strata Florida. Rhys had, according to the poet Guto'r Glyn, personal wealth which he sank into Strata Florida, although, as we have seen, royal imposition finally thwarted him. Morgan ap Rhys had begun as a monk of Strata Florida and in his 42-year service as abbot earned a reputation not only for renovating the church of Strata Florida but also for making the monastery again a centre of culture, learning and scholarship.

Both Rhys and Morgan also made huge efforts to restore the battered buildings, but probably in the context of a second decision taken early in the fifteenth century, perhaps even during its English administration, to reduce even further the physical extent of the abbey, limiting it to enclose its core buildings (Fig. 67).

One indicator of this rearrangement within a tighter curtilage was the building of a large agricultural storage barn to the south-west of the cloister ranges. Part of this is still standing preserved within the fabric of another, seventeenth-century barn. Details of this earlier building's original wall plan and beautiful ventilation loops can be seen in Figs. 68 and 69. The decorative nature of these loops may suggest they were designed to be seen by travelers along a road in front of the new curtilage which may at this stage have become a public thoroughfare.

Fig. 67: Plan of the abbey in the fourteenth and fifteenth century.

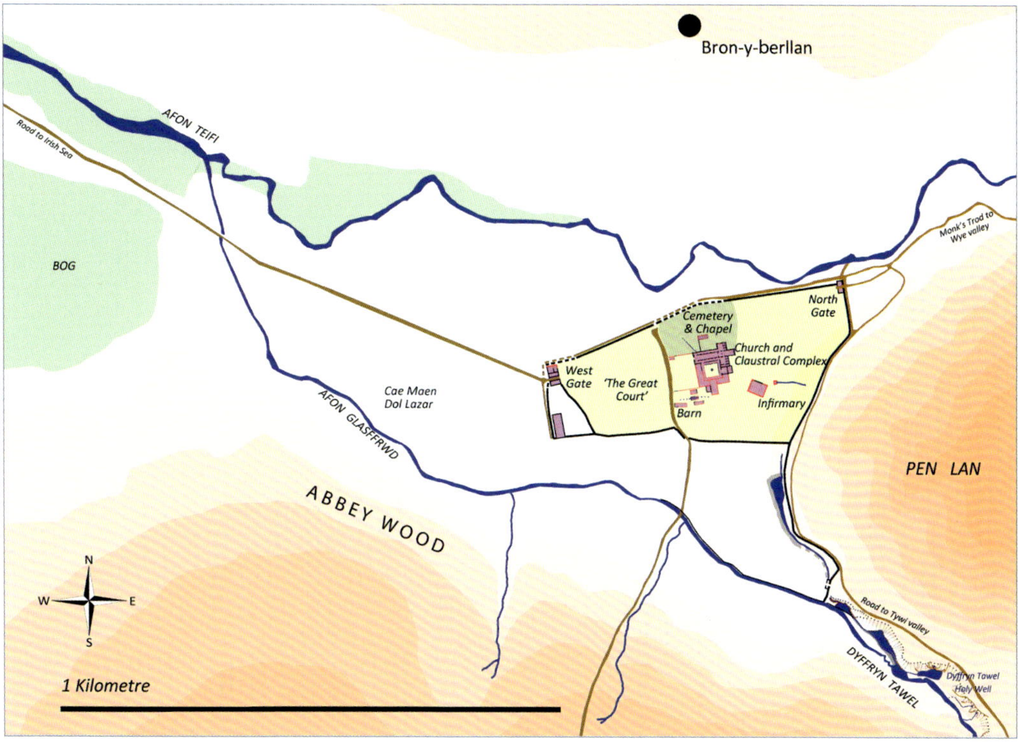

Bron-y-berllan

Road to Irish Sea

AFON TEIFI

Monk's Trod to Wye valley

BOG

North Gate

Cemetery & Chapel

Church and Claustral Complex

West Gate

'The Great Court'

Cae Maen Dol Lazar

AFON GLASFFRWD

Barn

Infirmary

PEN LAN

ABBEY WOOD

N W E S

1 Kilometre

Road to Tywi valley

DYFFRYN TAWEL

Dyffryn Tawel Holy Well

Fig. 68: Plan of the seventeenth-century barn of Mynachlog Fawr with the plan of the medieval barn partially incorporated into it.

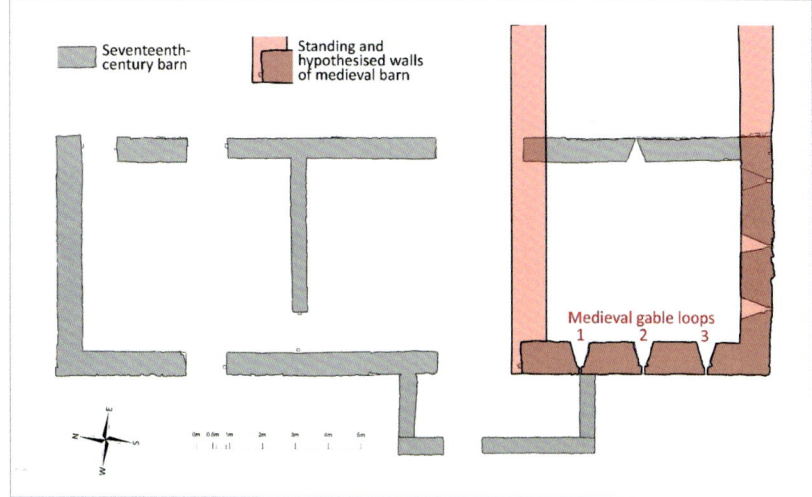

Seventeenth-century barn

Standing and hypothesised walls of medieval barn

Medieval gable loops
1   2   3

N W E S

Fig. 69:
Photographs
showing details of
the medieval walls
and ventilation.
They were made
from Dundry stones
taken from ruined
abbey buildings.

Excavations have already shown that the main gatehouse, probably in the later fifteenth century, was taken out of use and converted into a two-storey building described in a 1546 rental as 'one chamber above the Great Gate commonly called 'Penny Porth' with a little chamber under the same.. with two stables and two small buildings outside'. This would suggest that the large western end of the Inner Precinct, called the Convent Green in sixteenth-century documents, was also finally abandoned as part of the active monastery, although still visible to Leland.

We can also say that the extant remains of the church and cloister ranges show very little refurbishment in its masonry fabric. As happened in the early fourteenth century, most of the fifteenth-century improvements mentioned in the praise poetry were of fittings and not structure. There is, however, one observation made by Leland in 1538 which may also need to be taken into account here: he said that 'the fundation of the body of the chirch was made to have bene 60. foote lengger then it is now'. Evidence from the 1888 excavation of the church by Stephen Williams suggests that thirteenth-century tiling in the nave seems to have been removed at the west end (Fig. 70). Does this provide evidence for the abandonment of the three western bays of the church, perhaps left roofless? The length of these three bays is almost exactly sixty feet.

Fig. 70: Plan of the abbey as revealed at the end of the 1888 excavations, drawn by Telfer Smith. The tiling at the east end of the nave seems to have the appearance of its pattern being truncated at the west end.

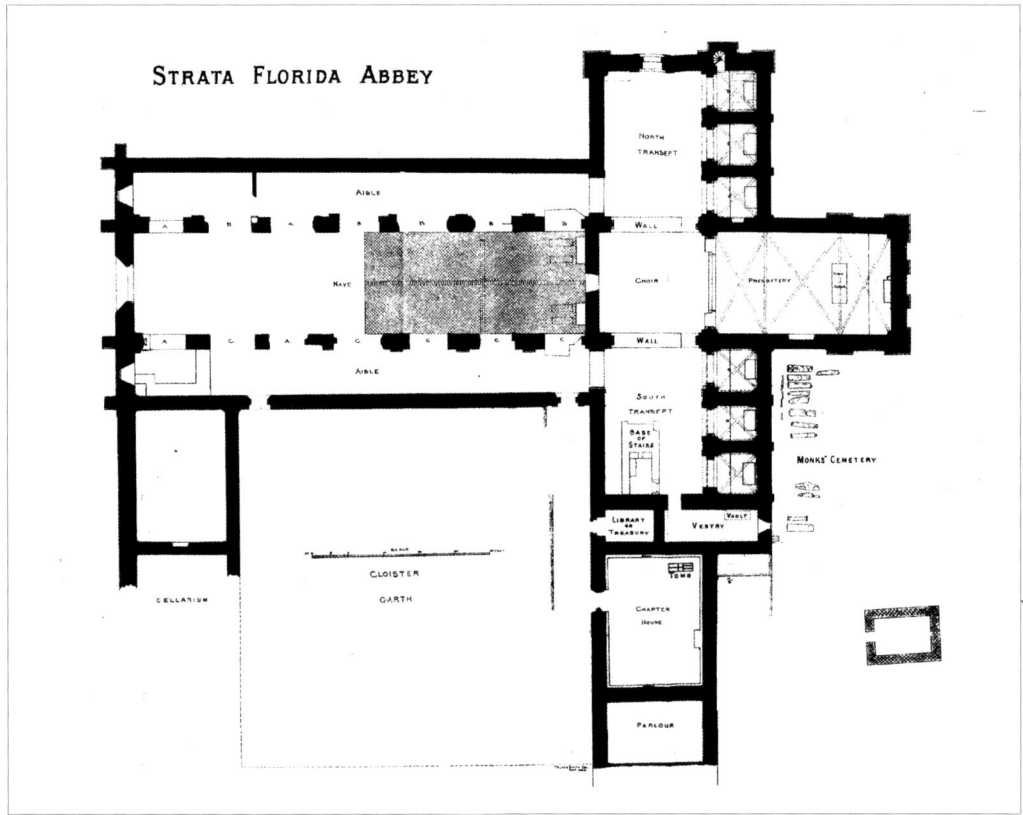

Throughout all this change and adaptation the abbey seems to have maintained its dignity. There is clear evidence that Strata Florida remained a prestigious place at least within the former bounds of Pura Wallia and the Whitland family of Cistercian abbeys, and that it maintained the 'Welsh project', supporting vernacular cultural production and an ideology of a distinct if not independent people. Janet Burton has recently pointed out, for example, that during the fourteenth and fifteenth centuries the post of Abbot was fiercely and bitterly contested on three notable occasions. The first was in the 1340s when some of the monks themselves, backed by local Welsh gentry, elected one of their own, Clement ap Rhysiart, while a rival, Llywelyn Fychan, was backed by others. Llywelyn, however, had taken control by 1347 and survived until 1380. The next contest came in 1383 at a point when the long, successful abbacy of Llywelyn Fychan had just come to an end. In essence the Abbot of Aberconwy, Johan (perhaps Ieuan) ap Rhys, once a monk of Strata Florida, claimed the abbacy of his former monastery, making forcible entry with armed men and archers and holding the abbey for forty days. For a third time, in 1441-2, following the death of Abbot Rhys ap Dafydd the abbacy was contested once again. This concerned another Johan ap Rhys, Abbot of Cymer, who claimed that Abbot William Morys, the incumbent of Strata Florida, had been deposed and that he had been elected instead. Why John ap Rhys made such an attempt is unclear, but Cymer by 1379 had been reduced to only four monks and the abbacy of a much more wealthy and prestigious monastery must have felt like a smart move. By 1443, the king had been asked to intervene and he promptly took the abbey under his protection, dismissing both William and Johan. Another monk of Strata Florida, Morgan ap Rhys, took their place and it was he who made a bold attempt to restore the abbey church.

These contests of themselves attest to the continued high standing of Strata Florida, with ambitious members of the Whitland family, senior members of the Cistercian Order, the Pope and the king of England all involved. Lurking behind all this, however, was a shadowy world of local power play among a gentry itself adapting to changes in the nature of authority and social order. One of the charges against Johan ap Rhys, for example, was that he had used the abbey seal (Fig. 71) to issue leases, probably to his local supporters. It is clear that all these claimants could not have acted on their own and must have been supported by those who bore arms and who were prepared to disturb the king's peace. In the end, however, it was always the crown which held sway, but the attraction of Strata Florida's reputation and long established place in Welsh culture led some to take a chance.

Fig. 71: The fifteenth-century common seal of Strata Florida.

The nurturing of that reputation led Abbots and their institutions to act as key players in the networks of their regional gentry and ministerial class, their 'affinity', which operated partially within the new English systems of governance, but also within the social practices and expectations of traditional Welsh lineage and social power. One aspect of this the Abbots excelled in: the patronage of Welsh bards and poets. Strata Florida was a leader in this, with its best abbots celebrated in poetry written by men deeply schooled in the bardic traditions. By the later Middle Ages these bards were members of a growing Welsh middle class of ministerial and court officials, administrative servants, scribes and recorders, historians, genealogists and writers, all locked into local gentry power structures. Thus the production of cultural items diversified and secular scribes now also produced manuscripts in the vernacular language, such as later additions to the Hendregadredd collection.

One man who seems to embody this growing complexity, but nurtured by the monastic engagement, was Dafydd ap Gwilym (c. 1315 – c. 1350), perhaps the most illustrious of all the Welsh poets of the Middle Ages. Born in northern Ceredigion at Brogynin, he was of noble ancestry and he is thought to have been educated in his youth within the walls of Strata Florida. He was a man conscious of the place of God in the natural world, but a man too of independent spirit and strong worldly appetites and behaviour. The tradition that he lies buried beneath a yew tree in the cemetery next to the abbey is based on a *cywydd* by another contemporary bard, Gruffudd Gryg (Fig. 72), but it is possible that Dafydd was still alive when that poem was composed.

All of this can only have been made possible by the incomes generated by the monastic economy of Strata Florida which seems to have been large in comparison with other members of the Whitland family, but not in the top league of contemporary monasteries even in Wales itself. There are two moments when we can most easily make this comparison: the records of the subsidy levied by Pope Nicholas IV in 1291; and the Valor Ecclesiasticus of 1535 when the Crown was assessing the wealth of monasteries. In 1291, the abbey was assessed at £98..6..4d. on a cultivated land area estimated to be c. 6400 acres and vast upland pastures. By comparison, the next most wealthy monastery of Whitland descent was Llantarnam, a daughter of Strata Florida, valued at £44..15s..0d., while the two richest Anglo-Norman foundations were Margam at £255..17s..4½d. and Neath at £236..1s. 5d. By 1535 the recorded figures do not show such a wide disparity: Strata Florida was valued at £118..7s..3d., Llantarnam at £71..3s..2d., Margam at £181..7s..4d, and Neath at £132..7s..7d. These figures do not always compare like with like and how they were constructed will remain something of a mystery, but they do show, for Strata Florida at least, that this was still a viable enterprise even as it emerged into the modern era when we begin to get a much clearer view of the landscape. Then post-dissolution owners surveyed and assessed what they had acquired, first in 1540 and 1546 and then at regular intervals into the seventeenth century. What, however, had been the journey, through the later middle ages, to this point?

The big changes we have detected in the physical fabric of the abbey and the contexts in which they happened give us clues, as does a close examination of the landscape. As the abbey began to face the new political and economic realities of the later thirteenth century onwards so the whole of society was making adjustments. That the abbey was forced to deal with these processes of change can be seen when Abbot Llywelyn was arraigned before the Black Prince's court in 1352 because he 'took to himself 60 tenants of the lord Prince of Cardigan and made them to be his own tenants by reason of which the tenants of the lord Prince were cast down and devastated in the realm of the lord Prince'. This was undoubtedly in the wake of a great loss of people working the Strata Florida lands, caused by the Black Death of 1349-50. By what process, however, these 60 families might have been induced to uproot and move from southern Ceredigion can only be guessed at.

In general the later medieval pressures came from more centralised systems of law, regulation of the economy, conduct of war, provision of state infrastructure and a whole host of other public commitments. This was all compounded and to some extent fuelled by shifts in the nature of European production and trade, leading to an increasing bureaucracy and, consequently, a growing and compounding capacity to impose and to take. Hard coin (Fig. 73) was the grease that kept this machine running, rather than the old patterns of render in kind and service. The increasing pressures to produce money put abbeys under stress and it did not help when monarchs, their officials and their companion elites saw them as 'fat cats' sitting on almost one third of the land resource of the realm, protected by rights and privileges given away in the early period of pious zeal and administrative innocence. The problem for the abbey at Strata Florida, as at other monasteries, was that the state constantly found new ways of raiding this perceived wealth.

Fig. 73: A gold noble of 1354-5, found in the gatehouse, where the abbey's money chests were kept. Its face value was half a mark (6s..8d), approximately 16 days wages for a skilled tradesman.

Thus, as the fourteenth century advanced into the fifteenth, the abbey's direct needs for in-house sustenance were being reduced by falling numbers of monks and an increasingly cash economy. This led the abbey to convert most of the in-kind obligations of land tenure into money rents and to release capital sums by leases to tenants for varying lengths of time which involved the payment of 'entry fines' or cash up front. This applied also to the abbey's own demesne farms which by the fifteenth century, if not long before, were being leased in the same way. This principle of converting productive capacity into ready money was also applied to some of the abbey's own activities, by selling to external entrepreneurs the right to 'farm' or exploit them. This included similarly leasing out the running of its sheep flocks and wool production, the use of its fisheries and mills including those used for fulling for a growing local cloth industry.

All this, alongside shifting attitudes to the exercise of authority and worship, changed fundamentally the ancient relationship between the abbey and its tenantry, previously based on kindred, personal obligation and the intercession of priests. It came to be replaced by the capitalist contract between landowner and tenant with wage labour as an accompanying system of production with its greater freedom and moral responsibility for individuals. As this happened so people bound by obligations were more able to make different decisions, whether it be to leave for the growing towns and industries or to claim land on the fringes of what had been traditionally farmed. This latter can be found in the countryside around the abbey in the gradual encroachment of farms and their fields onto the upper slopes of the valley, the *ffridd* (Fig. 74).

One final word needs to be said about the abbey in the Middle Ages. It was a monastery and the daily round of its occupants was based on observance of the Rule of Benedict as interpreted by the Cistercians. With seven offices spread throughout the twenty-four hours of the day, the order put an emphasis on prayer, study, physical labour and self-denial. It was emphatically idealistic in the beginning with a powerful reputation for piety and abstinence. The movement too inspired an intellectual and reforming energy which by the end of the thirteenth century had created 750 monasteries across Europe. Conventionally historians would say that these communities lost the purity of the ideal, that the energy waned and that its practices became as worldly as those of the Benedictines from whom they broke away in 1098. There is a strong sense of decline in this narrative, but the truth is that the world became more complex, as did monasticism itself with the growth of universities and the mendicant and preaching orders. Other ideas took root, including the notion of individual responsibility for redemption and a more direct and personal relationship with God, concepts which lie at the heart of Protestantism. The life led by the monks of Strata Florida in the later Middle Ages was still a continuation of the role of the spirit in an eternally sacred place. Because of their devotion that special quality of Strata Florida continued even though, in 1539, it ceased to be called a monastery as a result of Henry VIII's second Suppression of Religious Houses Act.

Into modernity: the Stedman years

The final years of the monastery were ones of constant pressure for the community under its last abbot, Richard Talley. It had been valued in 1535 by the crown and was, at first, identified for early closure because it was worth less than the £200 regarded as the benchmark for survival. In 1536, however, Talley won a reprieve by agreeing to pay a sum of £66 (100 marks), an amount he attempted to find by selling very long leases for abbey land. In February 1539 the final blow came and the seven remaining monks, including the abbot himself were pensioned off.

The documents provide us with a few glimpses of what it was like at Strata Florida in the closing years of the monastery. Perhaps the most striking are two conflicting witness statements taken in 1534 at the crown court in Shrewsbury concerning the very worldly crime of counterfeiting coins in the abbey itself. From these we can establish that the monks were living in individual 'chambers' with beds, fireplaces and cooking equipment and these appear to have been in the cloister west range. The statements also refer to the existence of other buildings nearby which included an ale-house and lodgings for the large number of secular people who seem to have had easy entry to most parts of the abbey. We know also that the three original gatehouses were also still standing, although probably pressed to other uses.

In terms of running the abbey and its estate, the relatively small number of monks relied heavily on secular officials who drew fees and no doubt other perks from the available resources. We cannot be certain how many there were, but the most telling indicator of the absorption of the monastery into the new secular worlds of the sixteenth century was the stranglehold on its revenues and administration taken by the aristocratic Devereux family. Walter, Lord Ferrers, was appointed in 1533 to be Steward of the abbey courts with, in 1538, his son, William, being made its Receiver-General with full control of the monastic resources. He was replaced in 1539 by his older brother, Richard when the abbey was formally dissolved by the Act of Suppression.

Under this administration in 1546-7, John Stedman, a member of a gentry family who were neighbours of the Ferrers in Staffordshire, was appointed as bailiff of the whole estate. By this time the Ferrers had gained an even firmer grip by leasing former Strata Florida property from the crown, including ten of the abbey granges. They also leased the area around the old monastery itself in 1547 called the 'Demesnes' still regarded as a distinctly different property from the granges and described in detail as:

> ...the house and site of the late monastery of Strata Florida.... and all houses, buildings, barns, stables, dovecots, walled gardens, orchards, gardens; our lands and ground whatsoever within the site, enclosure, bounds, circuit, and precinct being of the said former monastery; and all our lands, meadows and heritable property called 'Lez Demeynes landes'...

This demesne was bought outright by Walter Devereux in 1564 and comprised what became the core holding of the Stedman family when they, in turn, bought it from the Devereux in 1571. It is this which appears as the heart of the Stedman estate in a rental of 1577 (Fig. 74).

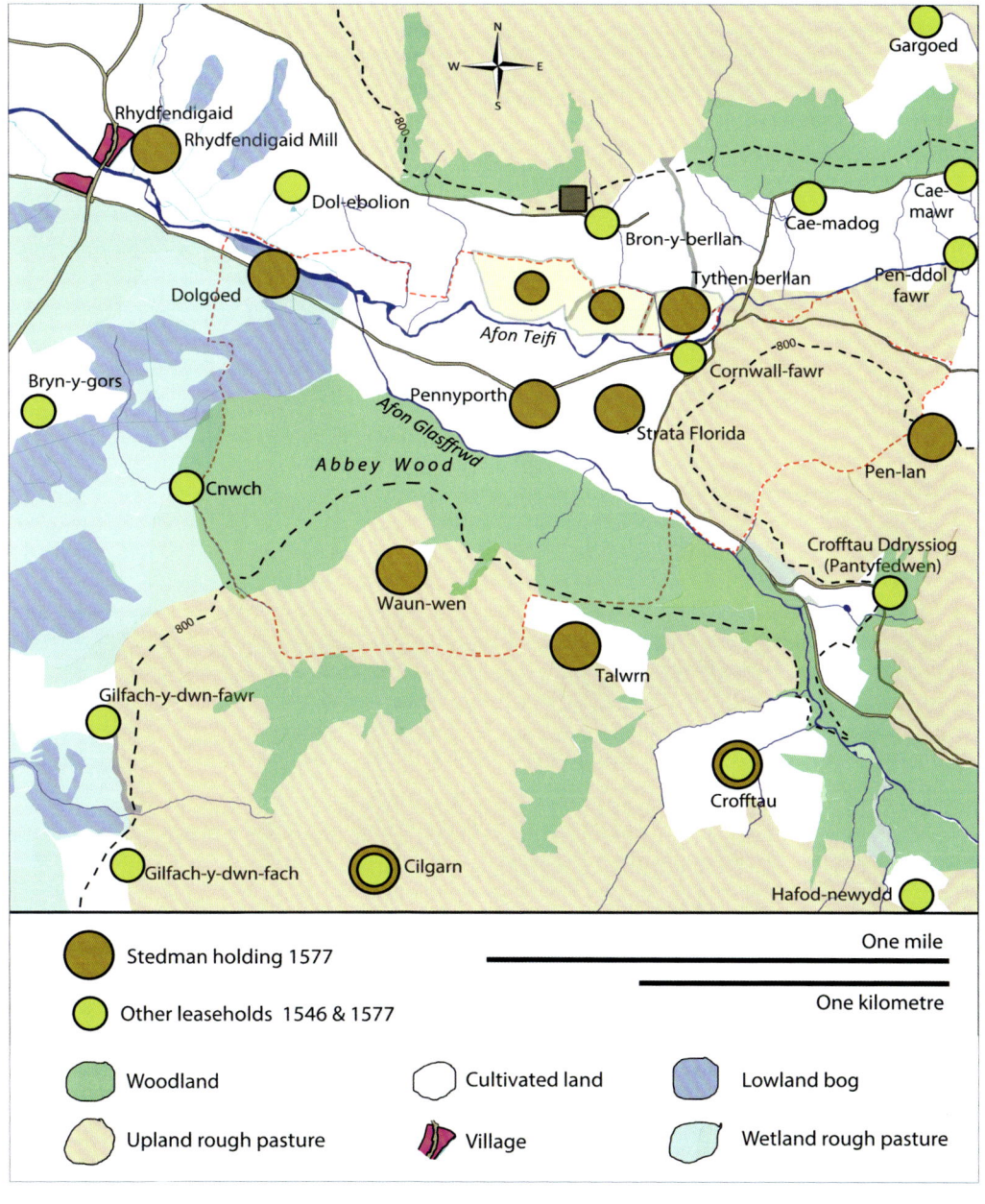

Fig. 74: A map reconstructing the disposition of the landscape of the former abbey environs as it was in the sixteenth century based on two rentals of the post-Dissolution crown estate in 1546 & 1577. By the later date the extent and nature of the late abbey's reduced demesne is identified because it was purchased by John Stedman. The ancient farms remained, but by this date we can also identify new farms which were probably established from the early fifteenth century onwards. These were taken from woodland and upland *ffridd*, pushing the boundary between *mynydd* and *tir* (enclosed farmland) above the 800 and 900 foot contours. The original cottage holdings on the wetland edge of Cors Caron had expanded and become full farms creating fields by drainage and enclosure. For the first time we can also begin to locate the houses (*tyddynnod*) of the rural poor. A red-pecked line shows the extent of abbey farm as it was on a survey of 1765.

The buildings of the abbey, then, did not simply disappear overnight, but were adapted to new world circumstances which had been emerging for many decades. There had been a gradual shift in attitude to land towards the modern concept of property, which was sharpened by critical changes in the laws of inheritance and property embodied in the 1536 Act of Union. This change happened, however, in such a way as it drew also on the configuration of what had gone before as well as a sense of the place's importance historically and socially. While it is clear, for example, that the 1547 lease to the Devereux family began to put into its hands the means of increasing yield, there was, at the same time, constant reference to the abbey and the integrity of its holdings, continuing to respect the legal instruments of the abbey, such as its pre-dissolution leases and suit of court. This continued well into the eighteenth century.

It may be that the 1547 lease was taken by the Ferrers to provide a home farm and accommodation for their new agent, John Stedman and his family. There is some evidence to suggest that the Stedmans lived in the western cloister range of the abbey buildings which, as we have seen, had already been converted into a series of chambers. This may well have included the western portal of the church as a grand entrance and completed the appropriation of the abbey's history and prestige. As part of this, but probably some decades later, the Stedmans created a large formal garden in which parts of the abbey ruins might well have been features (Fig. 75).

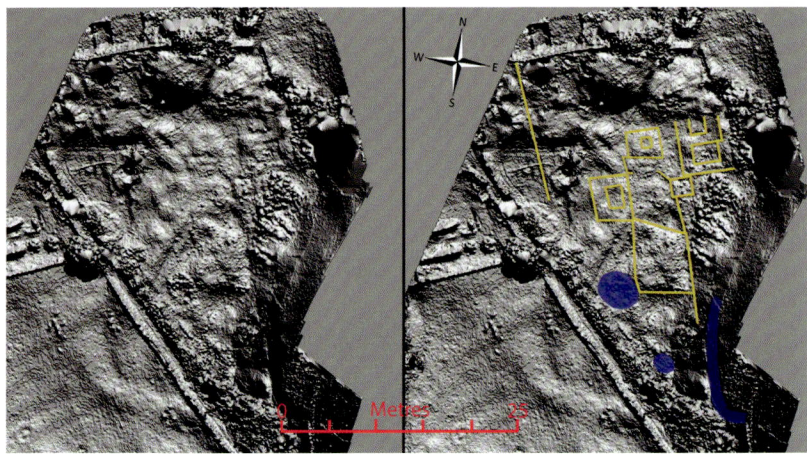

Fig. 75: Two photogrammetric images. They are complex and have several levels, but one element, picked out as yellow lines in the preliminary interpretation (right), is a formal garden of the early Stedman years around 1600. The blue indicates the remnants of its water-garden.

Recent excavations have also found that they constructed, out of the ruins of the abbey's refectory, a small ground-floor hall attached to this range, perhaps for formal dining. This was partially incorporated into the fabric of the present house (Fig. 76).

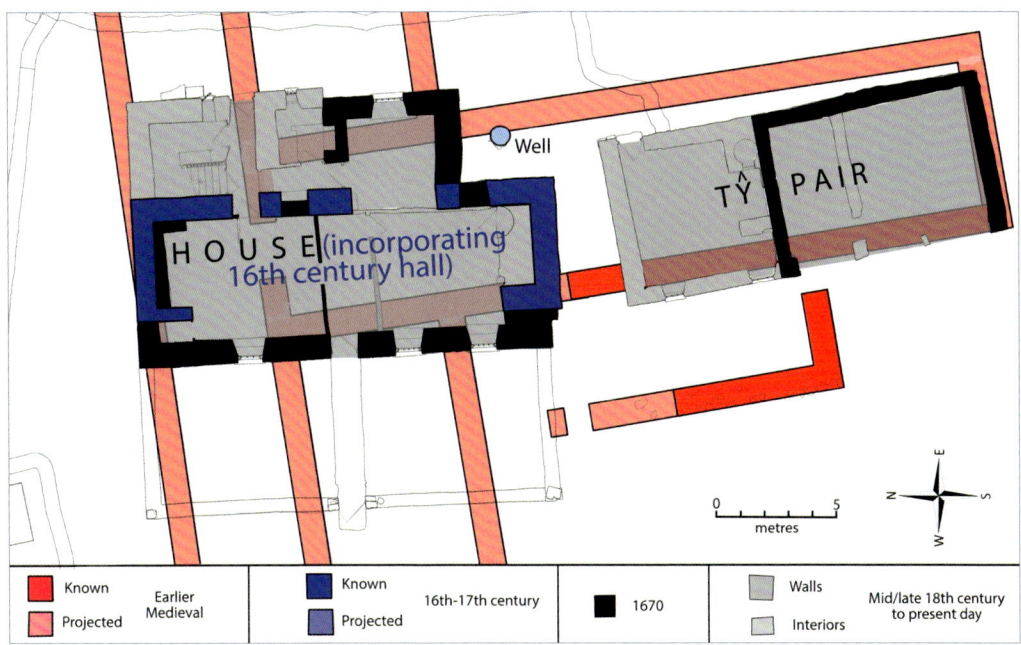

Legend:
- Known — Earlier Medieval (red)
- Projected — Earlier Medieval (light red)
- Known — 16th-17th century (blue)
- Projected — 16th-17th century (light blue)
- 1670 (black)
- Walls — Mid/late 18th century to present day
- Interiors — Mid/late 18th century to present day

Fig. 76: Plan of the sequence of buildings revealed by recent excavations beneath and around the house of Mynachlog Fawr.

By the time of the 1577 rental John 'Moel' Stedman had inherited his father's holdings and when he himself died thirty years later he owned property focused on the old Strata Florida core lands, but also spreading southwards into Carmarthenshire and Breconshire. His own son and heir, John Gwyn, however, who did not long out-live him, dying in 1613 at the age of 62, added a few more holdings to the Stedman estate (Fig. 77). John Gwyn's own heir, James, died in 1617 at the age of 28, but he had a son, another John. We can sense, however, from her will, also of 1617, that the strength of the family at this time lay in the figure of John Gwyn's wife, Margaret. She made remarkable bequests of fashionable Elizabethan dresses to her daughters and provision for her two sons and her grand-children, but it is the inventory to the will that tells us her character. By the time she died she had made her dowager life at Henfynachlog, the original site of Strata Florida Abbey, where she had built up an impressive dairy and cattle-breeding herd. She was, in her own right, a vigorous entrepreneur and one of the wealthiest women in the region.

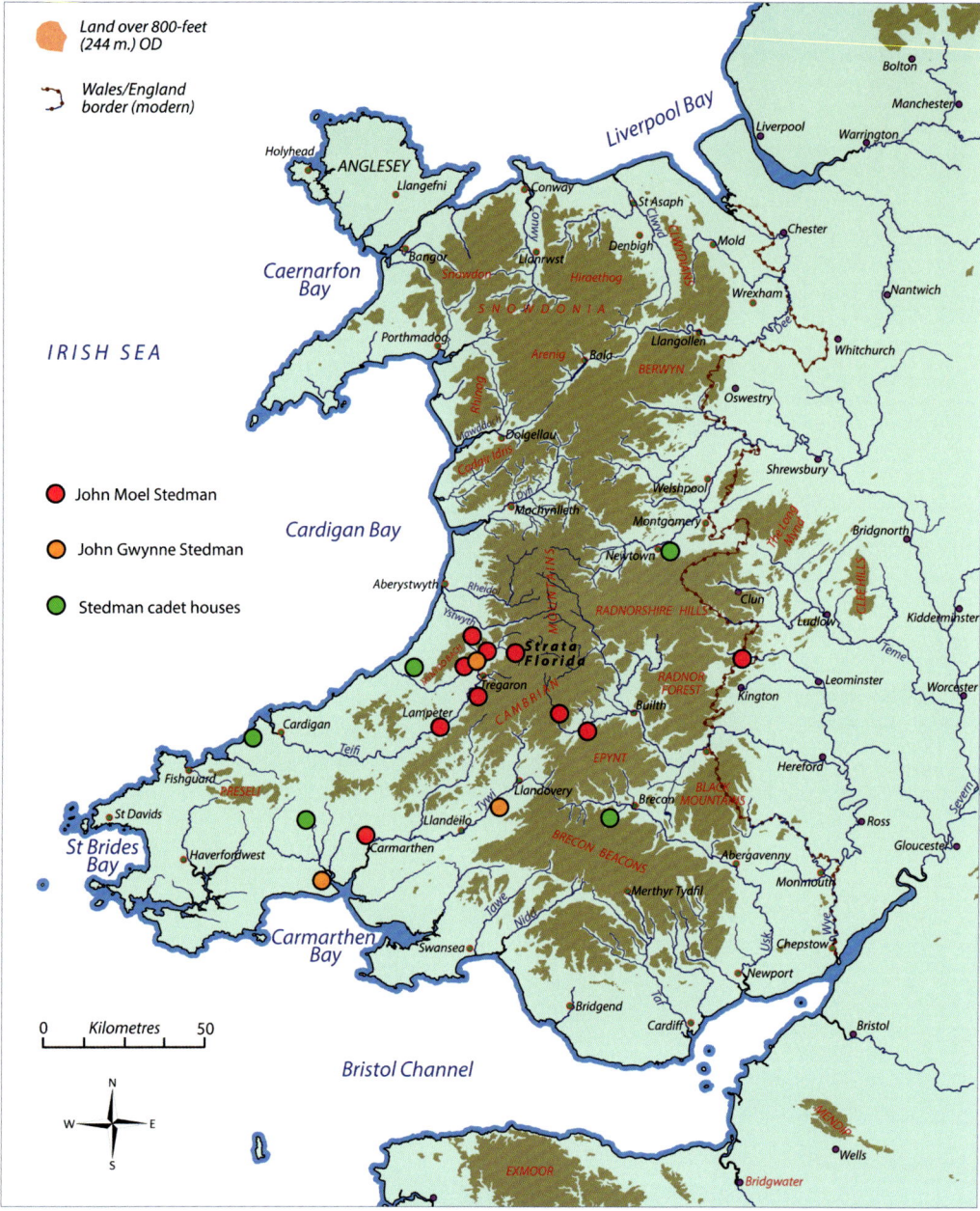

Land over 800-feet (244 m.) OD

Wales/England border (modern)

● John Moel Stedman

● John Gwynne Stedman

● Stedman cadet houses

Fig. 77: The Stedman property by the death of John Gwyn Stedman in 1617. The map also shows the houses established in the sixteenth and seventeenth centuries by junior lines of the family.

When his father died in 1617, John was only two years old and it was only in 1636 that he came of age and quickly married Jane Vaughan, the sister of John Vaughan of Trawsgoed. It was at that moment too that John Vaughan considerably raised the wealth and standing of the Trawsgoed family by purchasing eight of the main granges of Strata Florida from the Devereux family, by now Earls of Essex, thereby tripling the value of his property. He used part of this land to pay off the dowry settlement of his sister by giving John Stedman considerable property, once abbey land, in the upper Teifi valley, and this consolidated the holdings, some freehold, some leasehold, built up by his predecessors.

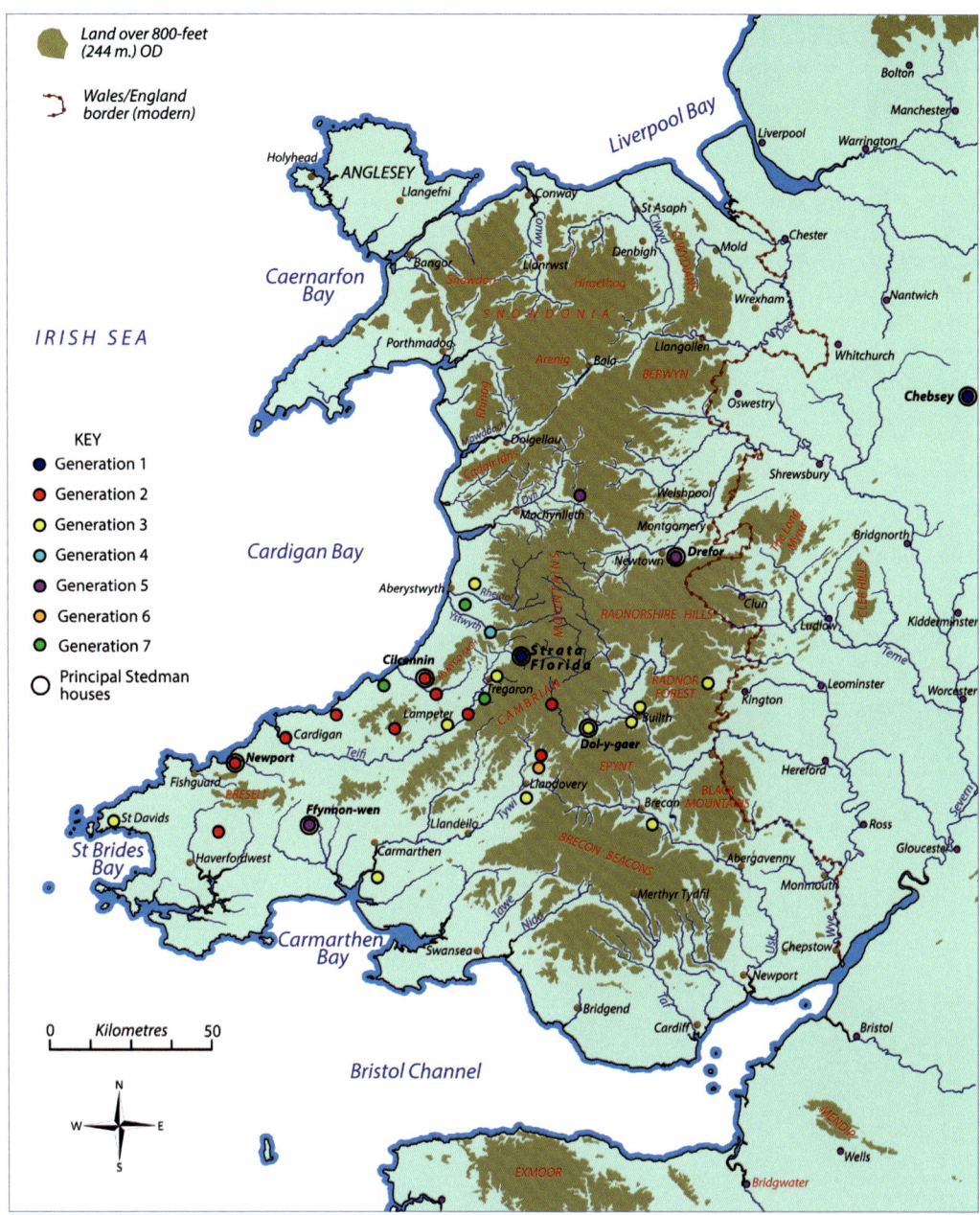

Map key:

KEY
- Generation 1
- Generation 2
- Generation 3
- Generation 4
- Generation 5
- Generation 6
- Generation 7
- Principal Stedman houses

Land over 800-feet (244 m.) OD

Wales/England border (modern)

Fig. 78: The marriage network of the Stedmans of Strata Florida from 1546 to 1745. The first three generations from John Stedman to John Gwyn Stedman were the most dynamic.

This was the high point of the Stedmans of Strata Florida. Over several generations they had married well, one might even say 'strategically', and their gentry kin networks were extensive and highly placed. This continued until the direct Stedman line ended in the mid-eighteenth century and can be mapped to demonstrate their world of connection (Fig. 78).

To show their place in this world we can record that the Stedmans had, on a number of occasions, been High Sheriffs of Cardiganshire and on ceremonial and smart social occasions Margaret's beautiful dresses must have been worn with distinction.

By the time that John Stedman died in 1649, however, the signs of decay in the family dynamic had begun to show. Perhaps drawn by the elevated status of the Vaughans and an attempt by Jane to keep up with her rising family star, debts started to accumulate. They are there in John's will and they were worse by the time Jane herself died in 1670. Although her will showed the growing debt it also demonstrated her ambition still to act as a women of standing, using money and property she had squirelled away and held in her own right. Despite the fact that she and her husband had lived for a time in a town-house in Brecon, her last acts also included a strong sentiment for Strata Florida. The nineteenth-century excavations recovered one re-used Dundry stone bearing an inscription in her name, probably a memorial set up in her garden among the ruins of the abbey (Fig. 79).

Fig. 79: Inscription commemorating 'JANE STEDMAN WIDOW 16** OF STRATA FLORIDA' carved on a piece of re-used Dundry stone from the abbey's architecture.

In her will Jane also left £200 for building a new Stedman family house which is the one now standing as part of the Mynachlog Fawr complex. This was the moment when the old abbey buildings were finally abandoned and the formal landscape of house and gardens completely re-designed. A survey of 1765 shows the general layout:

Fig. 80: Estate map of 1765 created for the Powells of Nanteos by John Davies (NLW Nanteos 302 132/2/4). Key: A. The house funded by Jane Stedman's will in 1670; B New barn; C Gentry Gatehouse; D Ruined Tŷ Pair; E abbey ruins; F St Mary's church; G Pennyporth — abbey main gatehouse.

The new house itself was first illustrated by Samuel and Nathaniel Buck when they published a view of the ruined abbey in 1741 (Fig. 81).

Fig. 81: A reconstruction of the 1670 house façade by comparing Buck print with recent elevation photogrammetry. The windows were moved to their current position when it became a farmhouse c.1800.

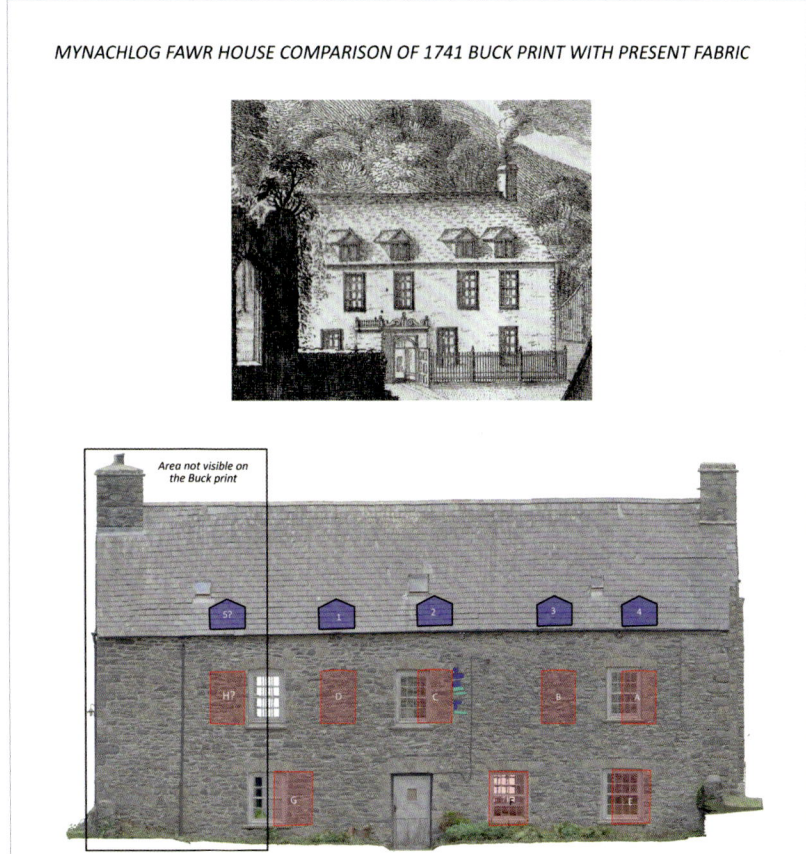

MYNACHLOG FAWR HOUSE COMPARISON OF 1741 BUCK PRINT WITH PRESENT FABRIC

The original floor plans can be reconstructed using architectural evidence (Fig. 82)

Fig. 82: The floor
plans of the original
house of 1670.

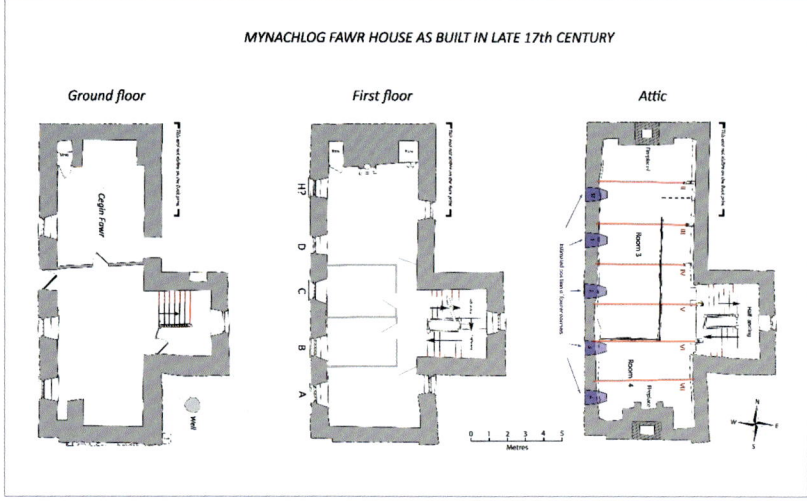

This must have been a much reduced dwelling for a family of the status of the
Stedmans and it is likely that they lived in other places as well. However, it does,
perhaps, reflect reduced circumstances brought about by the debt which never
went away but was rather compounded and increased over the final generations.
All this was itself made more difficult by a persistent trend for the Stedman male
heirs to die relatively young (Fig. 83).

Fig. 83: Early
death in the
Stedman family.

ESTATE HOLDER	DATE OF DEATH	AGE AT DEATH	STATUS OF HEIR
James Stedman	1617	28/9	heir in minority aged 2
John Stedman	1649	34	heir in minority late teens
James Stedman	1672	40	heir in minority late teens
John Stedman	1688	c. 32	heir in minority
Richard Stedman	1703/4	35	heir in minority
Richard Stedman	1745	early 40s	no heir

This was so for the last generation of the Stedmans of Strata Florida too. In 1723
Richard Stedman had married Anne Powell, daughter of another powerful gentry
family at Nanteos, and they had two daughters, Avarina and Elizabeth, both of whom
died in childhood and are remembered on a grief-laden slate plaque on the wall of
St. Mary's church. Anne Stedman's portrait (Fig. 84) survives, painted in her younger,
Strata Florida days. She had married again and moved away, but on her death in 1778
she returned to be buried in St Mary's church with her first husband and children.

Fig. 84: Portrait of Anne Stedman.

As a result of these deaths Richard died in 1745 without issue or direct heir and it would seem that his brother-in-law Thomas Powell had taken on the large Stedman debt in exchange for the Strata Florida estate. This remained nominally in Anne Stedman's hands until her death at which point it was legally absorbed into the Nanteos upper Teifi valley Sunnyhill property. Already, by 1765, however, the Nanteos managers commissioned a survey to be drawn of the 'Abbey Farm' (now Mynachlog Fawr). The plan serves also as a useful point at which to consider what had happened to the landscape around Strata Florida. For the first time we can also see the detail of how a valley-floor farm functioned with a regime of mixed cultivation and rotation (Fig. 85).

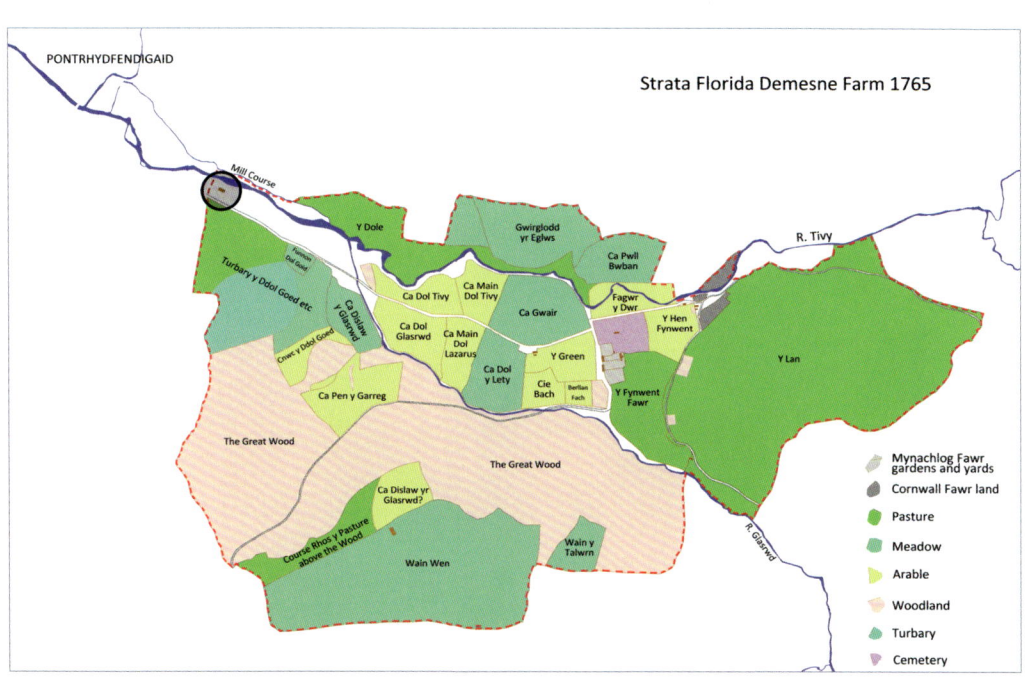

Fig. 85: Information drawn from the 1765 Nanteos survey and re-mapped. The location of the Strata Florida 'Old Farmhouse' drawn in 1888 by Worthington Smith for Stephen Williams (Fig. 86) is shown in a shaded circle in the top left-hand corner.

In the area around the abbey there was continuing expansion, with increasing populations bringing increased revenues for the landowners. The labourers on the estates, the successors of the bond tenants of the Middle Ages, were perched among the fields of the tenant farmers as can be seen on the 1765 survey and the environs mapping (Fig. 87). One of these was recorded by Stephen Williams in a famous illustration often used as the archetype of the 'Welsh house' (Fig. 86).

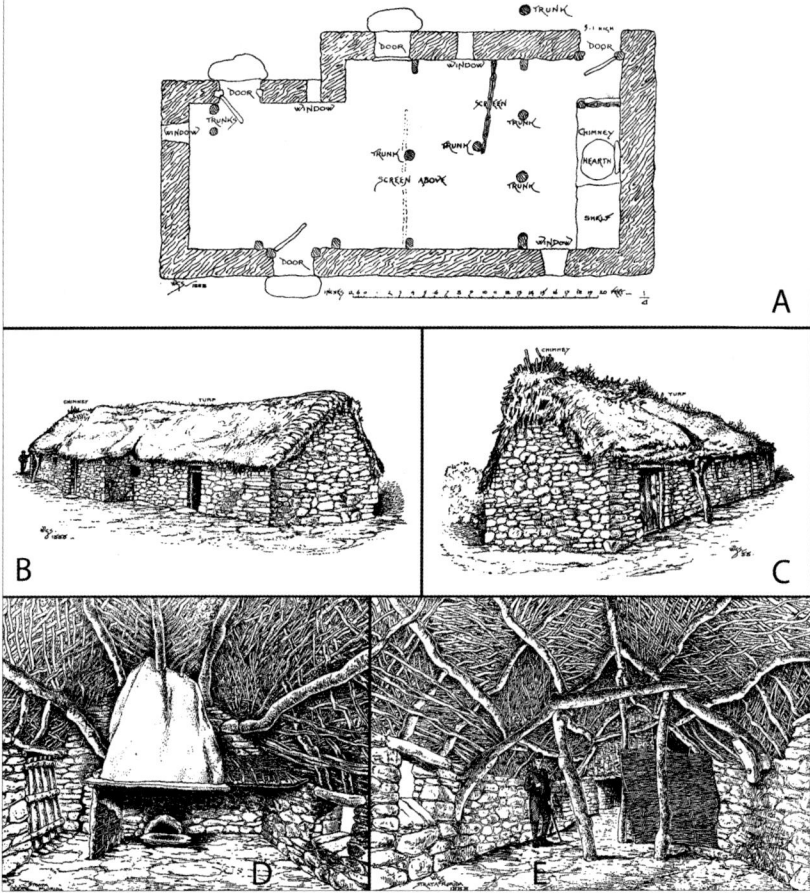

Fig. 86: 'The Old Welsh Farmhouse' recorded by Worthington Smith for Stephen Williams; this has since become an oft-repeated image of what a rural peasant dwelling of the Welsh uplands would have looked like.

Most striking on the map of 1765 is the presence of the poor and landless who had been forced to take pieces of the upland commons, the *mynydd*, as 'squatters' under English law, but as dwellers in the *tai unnos* (one-night-houses) by Welsh customary tenure. It is clear that Welsh bailiffs and administrators of the parish Poor Law sanctioned this activity and, for the most part, turned a blind eye. Increasingly these can be found in documents and can be mapped (Fig. 87).

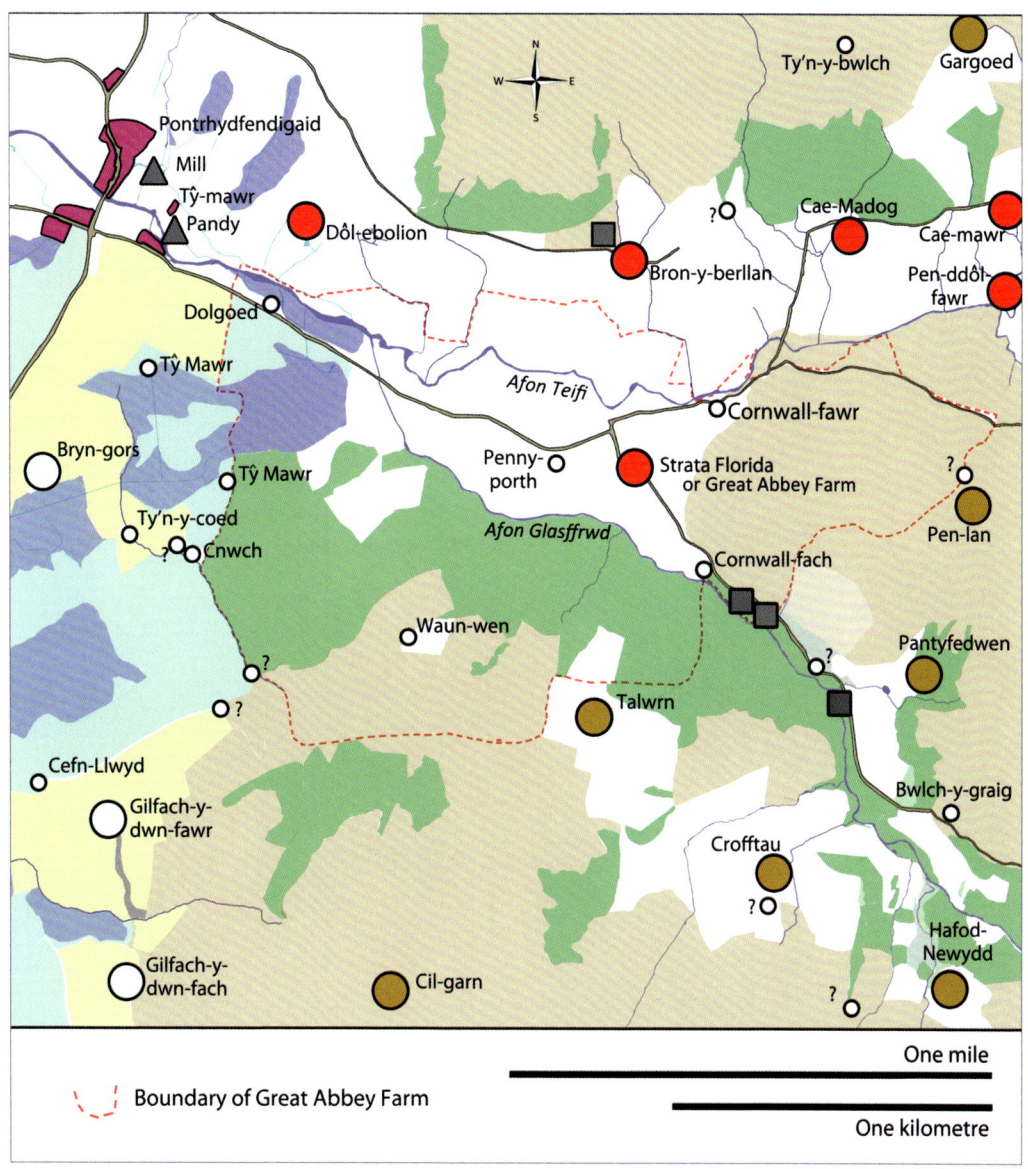

Fig. 87: 'The abbey's environs in 1765. By this date cultivation had expanded further with increasing numbers of upland farms being established. Woodland was also being eroded, and the wetlands were being drained and enclosed (yellow). Pontrhydfendigaid was expanding with the addition of a fulling mill (pandy). The abbey precincts and demesne had completed their transition into farmland with only the three original gates functioning as buildings. Both the northern and southern gates had been re-named as Cornwall (Cornel-y-wal, the 'corner of the wall', i.e. the precinct boundary). We can also see where the rural poor were living (small white circles) in *tyddynnod* (place-name Ty'n-) scattered throughout the landscape sometimes with small acreages of land around them for their own use.

What is not shown on Fig. 87 is the rapidly-expanding mining of lead, driven by the profit motives of the great estates and the Crown which had retained the mineral rights on some of the former abbey lands. Disputes between the estates and the Crown led to open violence at times as boundaries and rights were challenged. The estates, however, off the back of this wealth and the engagement of the landowners in the growth of world trade and empire, drew in exceptional revenues which funded many ambitious re-building programmes for mansions and parklands. For Strata Florida this income all went to Nanteos and not to any re-building of the Stedman mansion and surrounding landscape which are thus preserved for us today (Fig. 88).

Fig. 88: The house and parkland of Nanteos rebuilt in the mid-eighteenth century for Anne Stedman's brother, Thomas Powell M.P.

The acquisition of the Stedman holding had doubled the land area in the hands of the Powells, but they had also come to possess something that had probably originated in the abbey of Strata Florida itself: the Nanteos Cup (Fig. 89).

Fig. 89: The Nanteos cup: as it is today displayed in the National Library of Wales on the left, and on the right as it was seen and drawn by Worthington Smith in 1888. Much written about this object comes only from oral tradition or myth-making in the modern era, but it is certainly a late-thirteenth or early-fourteenth-century mazer cup, something found commonly in a monastery kitchen or refectory. It was a wooden bowl made of wych hazel with written evidence that it was used in the nineteenth century by local people of the upper Teifi valley who believed that drinking from it (and indeed nibbling the wood itself) would restore sick people to good health. Some well-documented cups of this kind were used in monasteries for specific and special ceremonies and were often embellished with silver chasing around the rim and on the foot.

The establishment at Strata Florida would seem to have been let out for a while as a gentleman's residence, for example to the local Nathaniel Williams, who was a prominent Methodist. On a notable occasion in August 1768 John Wesley himself, while on a preaching tour, stayed in the house as Nathaniel's guest. He would have seen a moralising painting on the panelling of the house's parlour, depicting the choice of youth between good and evil (Fig. 90). In 1773, however, Nathaniel moved away and Mynachlog Fawr became a tenant farm.

Fig. 90: Panel painting in the house's parlour, perhaps late-seventeenth-century, but moved later to its present position. Youth stands on plinth with Good, an angel, on his right and Evil on his left, portrayed as the devil in female form with the mask of deception and a cello to depict the sin of music. The inscription on the plinth quotes Isaiah: 'And thine ears shall hear a word behind thee, saying, This is the way, walk ye in it, when ye turn to the right hand, and when ye turn to the left.'

A time of transition

By this time in the later eighteenth century certain key changes, symbolised in some ways by the person of John Wesley himself, were happening to how the world worked for the people of the Strata Florida region. Up to this point, authority in the countryside was still largely vested in the local power brokers, the gentry and the established Church of England. Not only were their lineages long and their practices embedded deep in the social fabric of the countryside, but they acted also as intermediaries between the local and the distant state and its agents, much as the abbey had done. The Acts of Union in the 1530s had confirmed this disposition and the Acts of Dissolution had released the capital resource and revenues of the landscape to strengthen their position. As we have seen, old estates of the historic Welsh nobility and other freeholds, such as the Powells and the Vaughans, had been enhanced, while in-comers, like the Stedmans, were also able to be entrepreneurial and establish themselves among the regional elites.

One of the prices of this shift in the social contract, though, was the suppression of a Welsh identity, which had been so strongly pursued by the abbey of Strata Florida in its support of the language and culture of the countryside. The dominant ideology, espoused by state and gentry, was an English-language 'Britishness', imposed, for example, through legal instruments, estate management, education and the established Church of England.

By the mid-eighteenth century, however, public challenges to these structures were surfacing and these grew through the nineteenth. Some of them were new, but some were the re-expression of things we have already been following for millennia. One of these is the re-emergence of a more ascetic form of religious belief and practice in the dissenting chapels which, although inspired by national figures like Wesley, struck a chord with Welsh sentiment in the same ways as the Cistercians had. However, unlike them it was also socially radical and very soon became an important ally of more secular forms of resistance, in terms of both class and identity. Chapels began to spring up everywhere, three in Pontrhydfendigaid alone with outliers among the impoverished settlers on the mountain edges as at Rhos Gelli-gron, Calvinist Methodists serving and binding together the people of the *tai unnos* (Fig. 91).

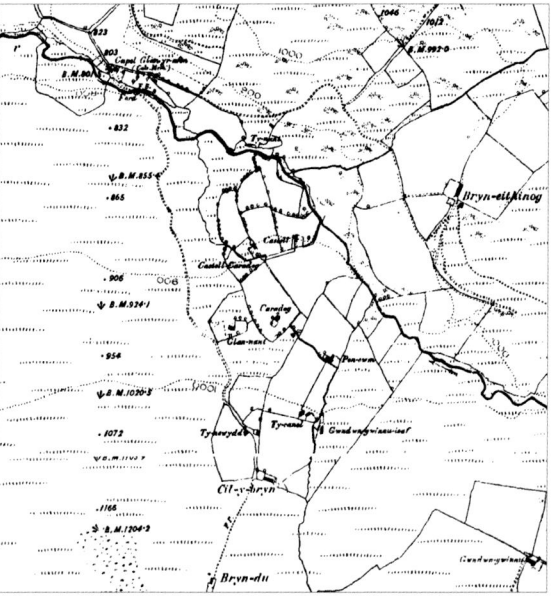

Fig. 91: OS First edition 6-inch-to-the-mile of the *bythynnod* ('huts') or *tai unnos* at Rhos Gelli-gron in 1886.

Some of their ministers, like the ancient saints, became heroes of the countryside, and in the moral and physical absence of their ancestral leaders they took their place among the gwerin working alongside the secular dissenters, politicians, writers and journalists, with their own ideologies of humanism, democracy, nationalism and revolution. They became the bottom-up voice of those who for generations had worked within the fabric of the landscape taking the daily decisions which delivered sustenance, stability, security and a settled way of living.

These are, however, gross over-simplifications which quickly become more complex when we look more closely at the detail of what was actually happening. It is unlikely, for example, that most people living in and around the former abbey would have been able or prepared to express what was happening in these terms. For many, the gentry was still seen as sheltering and protective and the landowners themselves certainly felt they were acting in the best interests of their tenants, albeit in a paternalistic and even condescending manner towards those with inferior education and simple ways of life. This is an attitude reinforced by the many visitors who began also at this time to travel into the heart of Wales to admire its awesome scenery and remark, in their journals, on its quaint rural folk. This was the dawn of tourism, driven by the invention of Romanticism, which, ironically, also inspired the greater awareness of national identity and ideas of social justice lying at the heart of resistance and change.

For a while, however, all might have seemed well and the status quo safe. The late eighteenth and early nineteenth centuries were good years for the estates and their tenant farmers. This lasted through the Napoleonic Wars and then beyond under the protection of the Corn Laws, when good prices were to be had for agricultural produce, especially grain. There are still traces all over the Welsh uplands, including on the hill of Pen-lan just to the east of the abbey ruins, where there are vast acres of narrow ridge and furrow ploughing reflecting this period of confidence and expansion (Fig. 92).

Fig. 92: The top of Pen-lan just to the east of the abbey ruins. The Napoleonic-era ploughing, called stitch-and-feather work, can be clearly seen with, in the centre traces of a medieval building to be associated with the abbey itself and the scar of at least one deep trench, a trial work to find (by 'fossicking') lead ore lodes.

This might have seemed a good time for the gentry and the established church to strengthen their hold on the tenantry by commuting the ancient exactions of tithe into money rent. This can be set alongside other actions of a central government delivered through the gentry: enclosure and withdrawal of ancient rights of communal access to resource, and the privatisation for profit by turnpike companies of the equally ancient rights of free movement along roads that had been in the landscape for millennia. These were all top-down actions and all were massive misjudgements which provoked increasingly violent dissent, such as the Tithe Wars and the Rebecca Riots.

Another central imposition which struck at the established social balances and altered attitudes was the radical alteration to the Poor Laws which had been in force since the Tudor period. Responsibility for the poor and destitute members of society had, for centuries, lain with the community through the parish with exactions made on richer people supplemented, occasionally, by the paternalistic contributions of the gentry, especially to those who worked for them. Such a system balanced the opposing attitudes of sympathy for the 'deserving poor' and of retribution on those who failed to help themselves. Within communities, and this can be seen in the parish registers, the poor and their histories were known, although families and individuals could be both favoured and stigmatised by collective memory. In 1834 the New Poor Law took this all away from the parishes and centralised it with the encouragement of workhouses, often in nearby towns like Lampeter, where the regimes were deliberately intended to make this the worst of all options for the poor who would then, it was believed, be forced into low-paid work. At local level this was softened by the continued support of charitably-minded people and other organisations, some church-based and some more secular. One device was the blind-eye turned to allowing the poor to take small patches of *mynydd* pastures or wetland *rhos* (moorland) to build houses as at Rhos Gelli-gron (Figs. 91 & 93).

Fig. 93: Photograph of a small cottage at Rhos Gelli-gron taken around 1900 when the small community had almost vanished as men, many lead miners, and their families left for the coalfields and other better-paid industries. This left older and single women eking a living from service or knitting or relying on the charity of neighbours. That there was also a spirit of defiance can be taken from the name given to this building and its tiny patch of land: Castell.

Thus changes begun in the previous century finally gained impetus through the nineteenth. The restriction on imports brought by the Corn Laws ended in 1846 and the growth of the world trade system started then to impact through the second half of the nineteenth century. Cheap foodstuffs came in from all corners of the globe, especially grain from the prairies of North America and meat from Argentina and the Antipodes brought on the first refrigerated ships. During this period too the Industrial Revolution began to bite, driven by new technologies and a profligate use of fossil fuels to be found in the South Wales coalfields. Populations rose exponentially, but largely in dense urban concentrations. Social and economic change was immense and rapid. Another element of social change was the growth of local education which had begun in the later half of the eighteenth century, but was still largely rudimentary as this description of the local school drawn from the notorious Education report of 1847 (the so-called Blue Books) recounts. The condescending tone of the inspector is obvious and we must be cautious as there was clear political intent in the way in which this was all written to denigrate the use of the Welsh language:

> The school-house is a substantial building on the road side to Strata Florida. It was built by the school-master himself, according to his statement. On approaching the school at several yards' distance, the buzz of voices sufficiently proclaimed the system of instruction pursued – every child reading its own book after its own fashion. On entering the school the noise was with difficulty stopped. Benches of the roughest description were placed around the walls. Some of the children were sitting with their faces to the walls, to which the books in some instances were fastened by pegs or nails, apparently as a preservative against dogs-earing. The floor was of earth, and the place utterly devoid of comfort.

By 1880, this school was replaced by a Board School at Strata Florida itself and was housed in the building which is now the entrance museum for the Cadw site.

For a while in the Upper Teifi valley the new technologies of industrialisation appeared to support local production with steam replacing the hydraulic power introduced by the Cistercians. For those in the lead industry, steam-powered pumps meant, for a while, that much deeper seams could be reached which had been below the water-table. In 1850, for example, the old abbey mines near Bron-y-berllan (Fig. 13) were re-opened and expanded to follow the ore-lodes which dipped steeply to the west. Florida Lead Mine (later Abbey Consol) became a big operation for about a generation (Fig. 94)

Fig. 94: Florida
Lead Mine depicted
on the first edition
25-inch-to-the
mile, OS map. The
drainage adits and
the spread of spoil
have left a legacy of
low-level pollution.

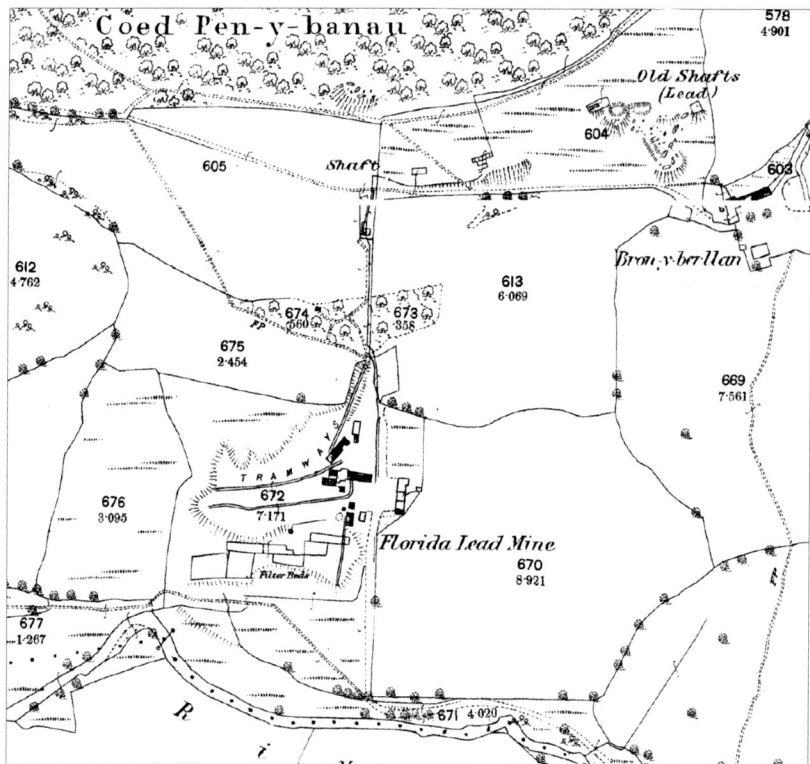

At the same time the more powerful weaving machinery driven by steam as well as
water was much more efficient and allowed for greater productivity in the woollen
cloth industry, allowing it to compete for a short period with the cotton mills of
England and the growing influx of cheaper imports. One consequence was that local
industry sustained the rise in population to be seen elsewhere in Britain. The village
of Pontrhydfendigaid expanded rapidly in the second half of the nineteenth century
taking on the appearance of a mining settlement (Figs. 95 & 96).

Fig. 95: The village of Pontrhydfendigaid by 1886. The old medieval *maerdref* core (red) with its corn mill and the location of the Tŷ-maer (Tŷ-mawr) had been expanded (yellow) south of the Afon Teifi with planned rows of miners cottages interspersed with the occasional larger dwellings of mine managers. There were also (brown) two large woollen cloth factories powered both by water and steam, with their own enclaves of workers' houses (especially Teifi Vale Factory). Serving this much larger community were a growing number of shops and two very large chapels reflecting both the religious and political sentiments of the growing population.

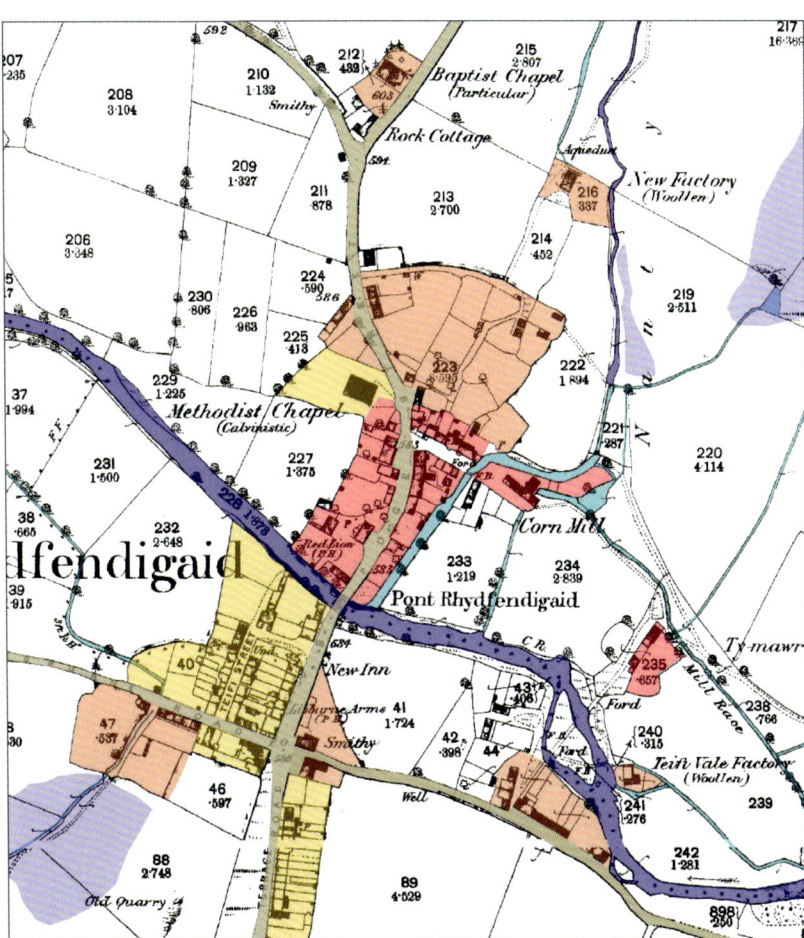

By the First World War, in the Strata Florida region, these old industries of cloth and mining had begun to fail before finally disappearing in the twentieth century, and it became more difficult for local producers on the tough soils and landscapes of the upper Teifi valley to compete with the rest of the world. At one time the drovers had taken great herds of animals eastwards to English markets, over the mountains along ancient transhumance trackways like the Monks' Trod. This too collapsed and when railways came into the upper Teifi valley in the 1860s it was the final blow. Skilled lead miners and many of the rural poor began to leave for the South Wales valleys and the rapidly expanding industrial cities with their new trades and modes of production.

Fig. 96: Miners' row at the south end of Pontrhydfendigaid photographed in 2006. One of the two-up/two-down terraced houses is pictured in the inset prior to restoration.

Up to the present: the Arch years

By the 1860s and 1870s a great recession in upland agriculture had started and a palpable retreat from the upland smallholdings began, rapidly accelerating into the first half of the twentieth century. The focus of agriculture once more retreated back towards the ancient farms. Into this changing world, about 1855, came Thomas Arch, a young man of nineteen, a farm servant who had been recruited from his previous life near Louth in Lincolnshire to become a gamekeeper for William Powell at Nanteos (Fig. 97).

Fig. 97: Thomas Arch the young gamekeeper at Nanteos and the Powell agent in his prime.

He brought with him a wife, Mary Anne, and new-born child, Hannah. William Powell must have seen great promise in Thomas because he made him Head Gamekeeper and in 1869 he became the tenant of Great Abbey Farm to serve also as the Bailiff for the whole of the Sunnyhill part of the Nanteos estates. In his time, tenants came to Strata Florida to pay their rents and face the questioning of the Powell agent who had become a highly respected figure in the farming communities of the upper Teifi valley. The rent table stood in the middle of the Parlwr of the 1670 house which by this time had been modified and expanded to serve as the home of a substantial tenant farmer (Fig. 98).

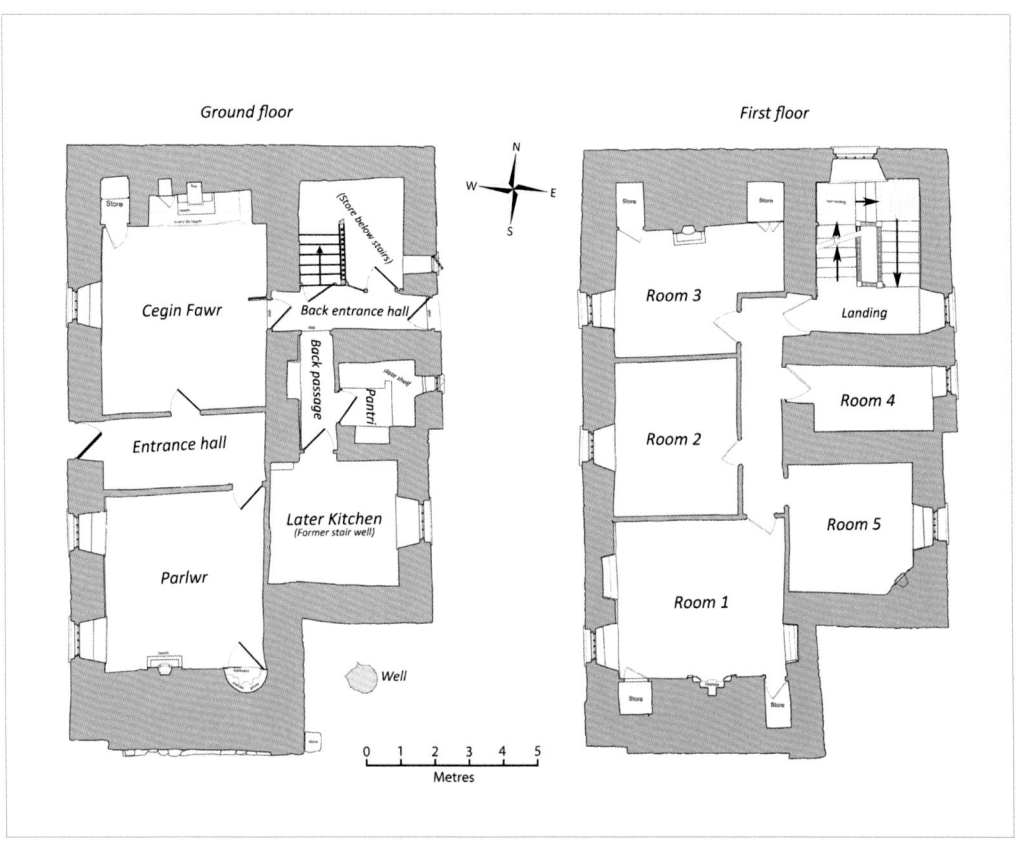

Fig. 98: Mynachlog Fawr house as it became by Thomas Arch's time and as it is today.

In his time at Strata Florida, Tom Arch met and talked with George Borrow on his journeys through Wild Wales, and he witnessed and assisted with the first major archaeological excavations of the abbey in 1887-90 undertaken by Stephen Williams. That too was the moment when the Office of the Ordnance Survey undertook the first mapping (1886) and publication (1889) at the scale of 25-inches-to-the-mile. On these maps we can see what Tom's home patch was like on the ground (Fig. 99).

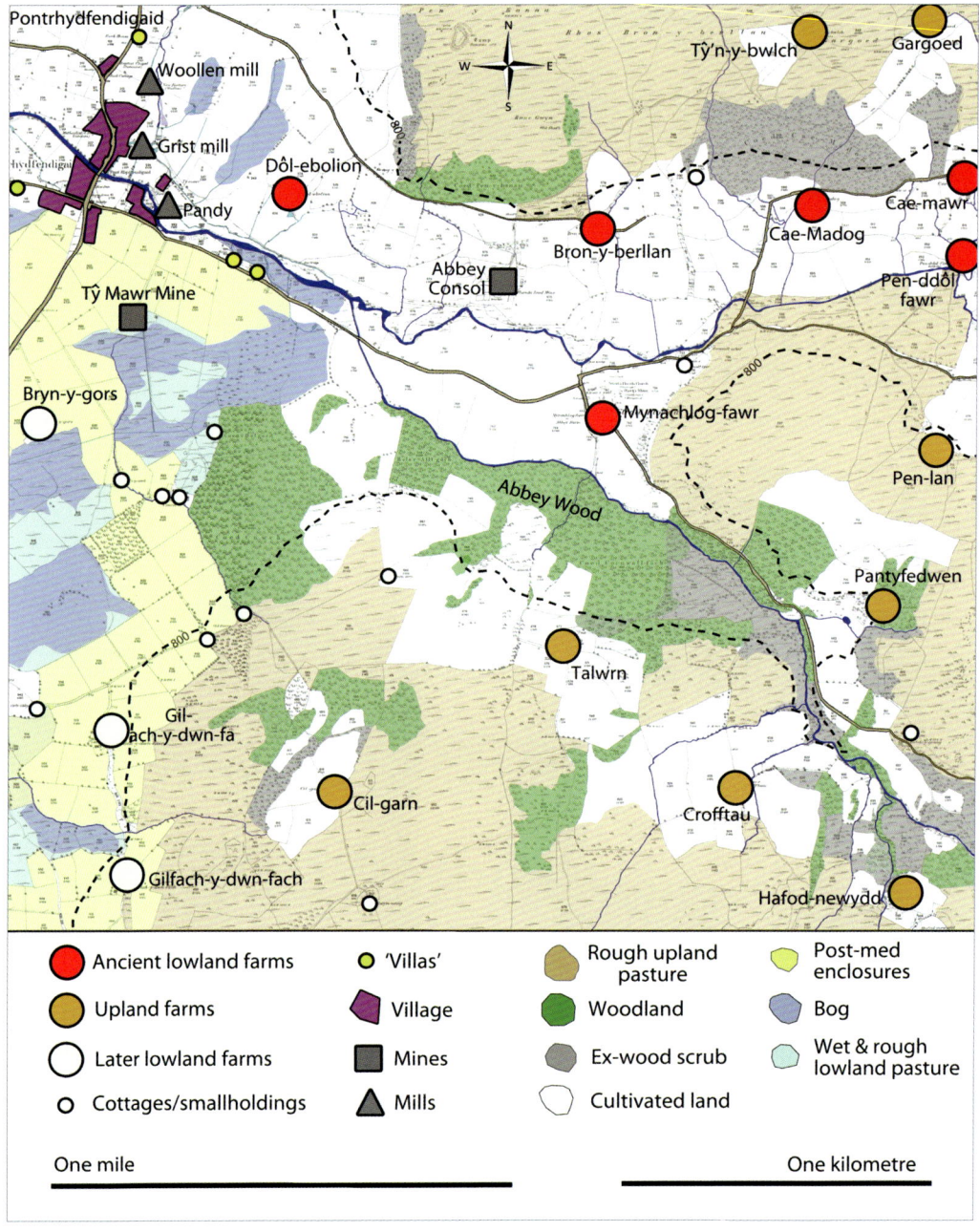

Fig. 99: The abbey environs as surveyed in 1886. Interpretation is put over the original 25-inch-to-the-mile OS map. This is the maximum expansion of the cultivated landscape at the point at which it was beginning to retreat. Upland farms such as Gargoed and Ty'n-y-bwlch would soon be gone, while some, like Pantyfedwen, would be converted to middle-class residences. These also were appearing in Pontrhydfendigaid which had expanded greatly in the 1850s to house the lead miners of Abbey Consol which was deep-mining the lodes first exploited by the abbey itself. Here too were the thriving Non-conformist chapels. What remains at the core of this landscape, however, are the ancient farms to be seen on the first map of the abbey's environs (Fig. 53). Together with the later enclosed farms on the wetland edge these are still the bedrock of family farming in this area as they were a thousand years ago.

Thomas Arch died in 1898, but by this time he had changed master, working for his last twenty years or so as agent of the Lisburne (Vaughan) family of Trawsgoed who had acquired the Sunnyhill estate from the Powells. As part of this the Lisburne managers had invested in a series of new farm buildings, creating a courtyard surrounded by farm buildings and diverting the public road between them and the house (Fig. 100).

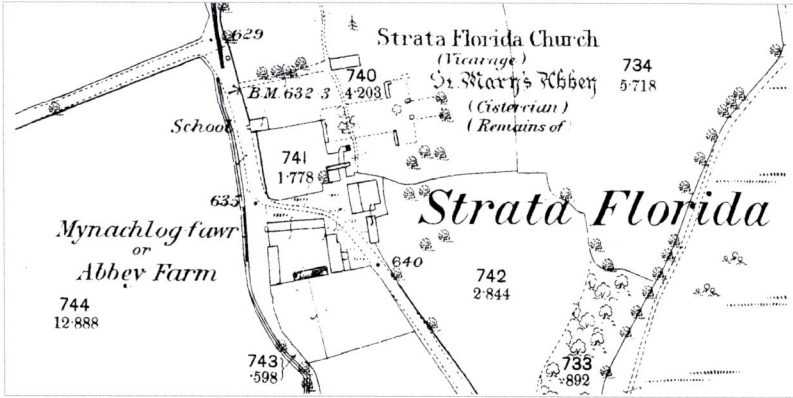

Fig. 100: Detail from the OS first edition 25 inch-to-the-mile map showing the new layout of the farm in the later nineteenth century.

Perhaps the most impressive of the new buildings was the stables on the north side of the new courtyard, built at a time when, although mechanisation was increasing in the agricultural world, the power source was still largely horses (Fig. 101).

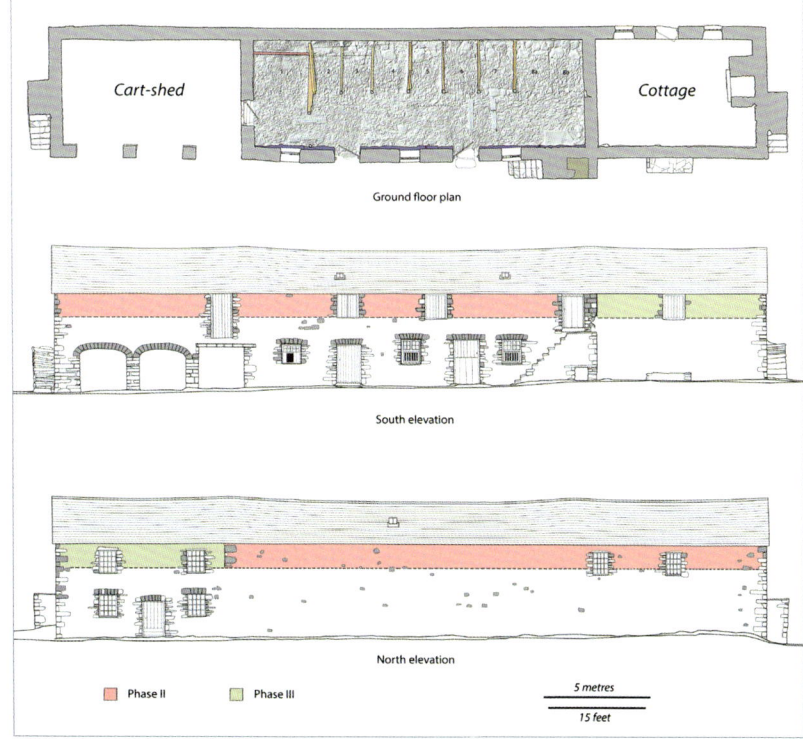

Fig. 101: Plan and elevations of the stables, built towards the end of the nineteenth century.

Despite this bold and risky capital investment in buildings, the Lisburne estate along with most others in the region could not stem the rapidly increasing fall in income and sustain the economics of a gentry lifestyle and social order. The First World War and its loss of heirs and men was also, for many, the final straw. In 1918, the Sunnyhill estate was sold, bought by a new sort of landowner, the capital investor. In the case of Strata Florida it was Sir David James, an entrepreneur with wealth derived from cinemas, London-based but with family roots in the area and a local home at Pantyfedwen. He was a paternalistic and benevolent owner, able to support and cherish the Welsh identity of the community from which he had originated. In 1953, he sold off most of the Sunnyhill farms to set up a charitable trust, the Pantyfedwen Foundation, but retained Mynachlog Fawr until 1982 when, after Sir James' death, the freehold was sold to the tenant, another Tom Arch, the grandson of the first.

It was Tom too who ushered in another change when in 1948 he bought the first tractors to be used on the old Strata Florida demesne. His son, Charles Arch remembered this moment from his childhood and recorded it in a wonderful book of memories about Mynachlog Fawr. The horses all but disappeared and the number of workers on the farm was gradually reduced. Coupled with the technology came another departure from the old ways, the abandonment of mixed farming and the introduction of specialist monocultures, curiously similar to the Cistercians in the twelfth century. Sheep or dairy farms became the norm and on the *mynydd* the old rhythms of short-distance transhumance between the valley floor farms and the upland common pastures were all but broken. It was local farmers who themselves completed the enclosure of the Cambrian Mountains to protect their livestock, so that it is now virtually impossible to roam freely as the monks and George Borrow had done.

Even with this intensive system of farming, however, it has needed intervention in the form of subsidies to make it viable, both from the British state and another European institution, the EU. This support has kept the countryside going, and was, up till very recently, designed to support the production of food, the honourable task of the ancient farms for millennia. The local agrarian economy, for so long dependant on the balance between the large estates and the efforts of tenants, freeholders and labourers, is now in the hands of the heirs of the ancient farms we have seen emerge from the mists of prehistory. Blown here and there by the winds of world markets, government policy and, now, conservationists, they have had to diversify even more than before. Once before, as we have seen, the monks of Strata Florida had diversified through technology and the introduction of the money economy. Even the poor of Rhos Gelli-gron knitted socks and tailored clothes for their wealthier neighbours and kin. Now there are holiday lets for tourists and local people commuting to work in public service jobs. It all continues to be a process of compromise, a tightrope between the bottom-up lives of those who live here and the top-down impositions of those who have the wealth and the power. It was between these two that the abbey and its community once stood. Today it is the elected councillors and professional officials of the local authorities.

What remains, however, are vibrant communities with a strong sense of the past and their heritage. A key element of this is the spiritual presence of Strata Florida, so deeply embedded in its landscapes and felt by both locals and visitors alike. That there is still a strong presence here today is due in no small part to the conservation and protection of the abbey remains by the state. The site has always attracted interest as an iconic place in Welsh history: the Cambrian Archaeological Association in 1847, for example, chose to visit Strata Florida on its first Summer School, even arranging a small excavation for the edification of society members. It was extensively excavated by Stephen Williams in 1887-90 (Fig. 102), and the remains left open until 1933 when, after considerable pressure, it was taken into guardianship by the Ministry of Works and its exposed masonry conserved. It is today run by Cadw, the Welsh Government's heritage arm.

Fig. 102: Stephen Williams (left-hand figure) showing a distinguished visitor around the site in 1888. The excavation below is of the south transept chapels.

The future

All futures can look either bright with promise or full of terrors, especially in times of change and transition which, in our world today, seems to be the constant state of being. Change in subsidy regimes, involving greater concern for climate and biodiversity, as well as rural deprivation and threats to language and culture are all things for upland people to worry about. There is no doubt that the people of the upper Teifi valley face considerable uncertainty and the prospect of more change.

In 2016, the Strata Florida Trust purchased the historic buildings of Mynachlog Fawr and now seeks to restore and convert them to uses which reflect the long history and meaning of the place. By 2021 we have restored two of these buildings and put them to new use, one (the Beudy) as offices and meeting room, and the other (Tŷ Pair) as a museum celebrating the life of Mynachlog Fawr and the Arch family. Soon we will turn to the Stables, Barn and House, together with a new accommodation building to become the Strata Florida Centre. The Trust will continue to work with the local community and its culture, but within a wider world, as the Cistercians themselves did. We will be drawing on the key narratives outlined in this book and building on its potential as a centre for Welsh history and culture, preserving, educating and offering a place for spiritual and economic well-being, as the abbey had once done to princes, paupers and pilgrims alike (Fig. 103).

Fig. 103: A late medieval pilgrim's ampulla cover found in the abbey gatehouse where those seeking salvation and solace would first arrive. An ampulla would contain holy water gathered from some venerated source. Made of lead, the front (left) depicts the scallop of Santiago de Compostella, by this time a general symbol of pilgrimage, and the back (right) a stylized heraldic device of no clear meaning.

Further reading

Arch, C. 2005, *Byw dan y Bwa*, Caernarfon: Gwasg Gwynedd (English translation: Life beneath the Arch, Talybont: Y Lolfa)

Burton, J & Stober, K. (eds) 2013, *Monastic Wales, New Approaches*, Cardiff: University of Wales Press

Davies, J. 1993, *A History of Wales*, Harmondsworth: Penguin

Johnston, D. 2017, *The Literature of Wales*, Cardiff: UWP

Robinson, D.M. & Platt, C. 2007, *Strata Florida [and] Talley Abbey*, 3rd. ed. (rev.) Cardiff: Cadw

Robinson, D.M. 2006, *The Cistercians in Wales, Architecture and Archaeology 1130–1540*, London: Society of Antiquaries

Williams, D.H. 2001, *The Welsh Cistercians*, Leominster: Gracewing

Acknowledgements

The author would like to acknowledge the contribution made to the Strata Florida Project over the last twenty years and more by countless numbers of students, volunteers, staff, friends and family. Each and every one has had an input into this deep study of an historic monastery set within its ancient landscapes. I would like to mention in particular two scholars who have been engaged with the research from the start and been constant companions on the journey: Dr Jemma Bezant and Quentin Drew. I am immensely grateful to them as I am also to Professor Janet Burton whose expertise on Welsh and European monasticism, especially the Cistercians, has been both an inspiration and a support to our work. I would like to thank also Professor Dafydd Johnston for his encouragement and guidance in the making of this book and for guiding me through the complexities of medieval Welsh culture. Father Brendan O'Malley too gave me valuable advice about the life of a monk and deep insights into the spiritual meaning of the monastery and its works, and I want to thank him for that. I want also to express my gratitude to the individual Trustees of the Strata Florida Trust, both past and present, who have supported and carried forward the vision for the future. Here I would mention in particular Professor Roger Earis whose guidance and friendship was so important, especially in the darker hours. Most of all, however, I want to thank my wife, Gaenor Parry, for her total commitment to this project and for her constant support and aid.

The Strata Florida Trust would itself like to thank the Welsh Government for financial assistance towards the production and publication of this book through the Wales Cultural Recovery Fund. It is also grateful for a grant given for the same purpose by the Sacred Landscapes of Medieval Monasteries Project funded by the Arts and Humanities Research Council as part of the Landscape Decisions Programme of UK Research and Innovation.

Fig. 104: The sculpture of the Pilgrim with its creator, Glenn Morris. Erected as a temporary structure in 2012, it finally succumbed to the elements in 2019. A community group is raising the funds for the artist to make a replacement of what has become an essential icon of Strata Florida and all that it means.

Illustrations: permissions and copyrights